Taking the Initiative

Supporting the sexual rights of disabled people

The Joseph Rowntree Foundation has supported this project as part of its programme of research and innovative development projects, which it hopes will be of value to policy makers, practitioners and service users. The facts presented and the views expressed in this report, however, are those of the authors and not necessarily those of the Foundation.

Taking the Initiative

Supporting the sexual rights of disabled people

Hilary Brown and Clare Croft-White
with **Chris Wilson and June Stein**

RESEARCH *INTO* PRACTICE

Taking the Initiative

Hilary Brown and Clare Croft-White *with* Chris Wilson and June Stein

Published for the Joseph Rowntree Foundation by:

Pavilion Publishing (Brighton) Ltd
8 St George's Place
Brighton, East Sussex BN1 4GB
Telephone: 01273 623222
Fax: 01273 625526
Email: pavpub@pavilion.co.uk
Website: www.pavpub.com

The Joseph Rowntree Foundation
The Homestead
40 Water End, York YO3 6LP
Telephone: 01904 629241

First published 2000.

© Pavilion Publishing/Joseph Rowntree Foundation, 2000.

Hilary Brown and Clare Croft-White with Chris Wilson and June Stein have asserted their rights in accordance with the *Copyright, Designs and Patents Act 1988* to be identified as the authors of this work.

ISBN 1 84196 005 5

All rights reserved. No part of this work may be reproduced in any form or by any means, photocopying, mechanical, recording or otherwise, without the prior permission in writing from the publisher with the following exception: the work may be photocopied, providing that all pages are reproduced in their entirety including the copyright acknowledgement and used solely by the person or organisation purchasing the original publication.

A catalogue record for this book is available from the British Library.

Editor: Liz Mandeville
Design and typesetting: Stanford Douglas
Cover photo: Saâdia Neilson
Printing: Paterson Printing (Tunbridge Wells)

Contents

Part One	**Acknowledgments**	1
	About this report	2
	The report's aims	3
	The challenges	4
	Finding your way around the report	4
	Scope and terminology	5
Part Two	**What do disabled people want from services?**	9
	The starting position	9
	Stop position	9
	Polite position	10
	Go-ahead position	11
	Quality indicators in a 'go-ahead' service	13
	Supporting the sexual rights of disabled people: quality indicators	15
	Current service responses	22
	Being clear about who is in charge	25
	User involvement	28

© Pavilion Publishing/Joseph Rowntree Foundation, 2000

Part Three	Why are these things important to disabled people?........................31
	A rights perspective........................31
	What is 'disability' anyway?................32
	And what is 'sex'?........................36
	'Coming out' and acknowledging differences . 37
	Personal as well as social issues............38
	Overcoming the legacy of institutional attitudes........................40
	Different issues as well as common ground . . 42
	Issues for disabled gay men and lesbians 45
	Issues for Black disabled people............47
	Conclusions 49
Part Four	Working towards good practice 51
	A rights perspective........................52
	Role models to inspire disabled people and challenge society 58
	Services that enable disabled people to exercise responsibility 60
	Inclusiveness across a range of services 64
	Staff roles which emphasise assistance 72
	Review and openness.....................79

Part Five	**Some tools for change** 83
	The inclusiveness grid. 85
	Using the six Rs to review your service 87
	Developing a policy document 92

Part Six	**Summary of key messages**. 99

Part Seven	**How we worked together** 103
	Disabled people doing research, not being researched. 103
	The methodology. 104
	The development of criteria for good practice 107

Part Eight	**Acknowledgments** 109
	The core group. 109
	The research team 114
	Services visited and consulted. 116
	Support for the project 117
	References. 118

Forewords

'When disabled people ask about sex what they hear is silence'
Morgan Williams SPOD, 1998

'Ultimately, disabled people enter relationships out of the strength of their own identities as persons with disabilities'
Longmore, 1987

Dedication

During the writing of the report the project group were saddened to hear of the death of Mildrette Hill. Mildrette campaigned tirelessly on behalf of Black disabled people and we would like to dedicate this report to her memory.

Part One
Introduction

Acknowledgments

This report has been written after extensive consultation with disabled people and their networks. It was produced with funding from the Joseph Rowntree Foundation at the School of Health and Social Welfare, Open University and has been written by Hilary Brown and Clare Croft-White with Chris Wilson and June Stein. The report is based on the expertise and analysis of a core group of disabled people who met during 1997–8, many of whom represented wider networks of disabled people. Members of this group visited services with the authors and developed an analysis of where services stood when it came to supporting the sexual rights of disabled people. This group and the services they put us in touch with are listed at the back of the report. Quotations from core group members are included in boxes throughout the report.

We have also cross-referenced our ideas and priorities against two recent books documenting the views of disabled people: one edited by Tom Shakespeare, Kath Gillespie-Sells and Dominic Davies (Shakespeare *et al.*, 1996) which analyses the views of disabled men and women on gender and sexuality and the other edited by Gillespie-Sells, Hill and Robbins (Gillespie-Sells *et al.*, 1998) documenting research by disabled women on women's sexuality issues. We should like to acknowledge the contribution these works made to our thinking.

Part One Introduction

About this report

This report is designed to provide an overview of issues facing disabled people in relation to sexuality and personal relationships, and of positive service initiatives designed to address them. It sets out to review these issues and to identify priorities for research and service development. It describes the legacy of segregated schooling, patronising attitudes and institutional provision, for individuals and for services. In opposition to this legacy, criteria for good practice which emphasise user involvement and empowerment were drawn up to act as a guide when evaluating provision with users and providers of services. These indicators are set out with discussion about how far current practice reflects the aspirations of disabled people. We have also drawn on the literature about sexuality and disability. From this a suggested agenda for service development has been set out.

The project considered how these principles should be applied across all service provision, including sex education, personal assistance in residential and domiciliary settings and access to generic and specialised counselling, contraception and fertility services.

The report's aims

The report has six aims:

1   to review current thinking about sexuality and disability
2   to identify the aspirations of disabled people – what they really want – and the issues which face them in relation to the services they are offered

3   to establish criteria for service quality derived from disabled people's analysis and first-hand experience

4   to take stock of current practice and progress towards disabled people's goals

5   to set out what good practice would look like in a range of service settings

6   to develop an agenda for service development and research.

The report is written for a diverse audience, since these issues are of concern to all agencies which serve disabled people and, within these agencies, are of interest to users, staff, managers, funders and policy-makers. It is intended to inform service users about what they can expect and ask for, and to inspire disabled people to set up their own services and networks as well as to take a more vocal and influential role around these issues in professionally-led and mainstream agencies. The report seeks to challenge service providers whose attitudes and beliefs often lead to services and structures which undermine, rather than underpin, autonomy for disabled people.

The challenges

The report seeks not only to galvanise disabled people, but also to challenge in a fundamental way all readers whose views about sexuality (reflecting those of society at large) may confine, exclude and oppress disabled people and in doing so diminish us all.

Part One Introduction

This report aims to challenge the views of non-disabled readers about:

- what disables people; they are often more disabled by society's reactions and failure to provide services or ways for them to be included than they are by their specific impairment

- what it means to be 'normal', 'attractive' and 'good-looking' and how our narrow interpretations limit many people, not only those who are obviously 'disabled'

- what it means to 'have' sex, or to 'be' sexual, and how limited and limiting a narrow view can be

- what services people want and how they can be delivered in ways which allow them to take and then keep control of their lives

- how helpful 'helpful' people really are and what right others have to intervene/ interfere in the sexual lives of individuals or the politics of disabled people.

Finding your way around the report

Following this introductory chapter which sets out the aims and scope of the report: **Part 2** sets out what it is that disabled people really want from society and from services to underpin rather than undermine their sexual rights. This section ends with a list of criteria – the six Rs, which summarises these aspirations in the form of a charter listing criteria which can be applied to a range of services.

Part 3 steps back and analyses why these are the key issues and how they have grown out of an increasing body of disabled people's thinking, activism and literature.

Part 4 returns to the practical and takes stock of current service provision, using the six Rs criteria.

Part 5 offers some tools for change, ideas to help you work on these issues in an organisation or network you belong to yourself: a way of plotting your attitudes and values on a grid, a checklist for reviewing your own services and a set of headings to start you on a discussion about what should be in any policy document for your agency.

Later sections of the report include a summary of the main points, references and a short section on how we worked together, which might be useful for others working on this kind of collaborative project.

Scope and terminology

This report is written primarily about the experiences of people with physical and sensory impairments. Of course there is much common ground with the way services have addressed issues for people with learning disabilities and those with mental health problems, but there are also important distinctions to be made.

Unlike people with learning disabilities and people who use mental health services, disabled people have not taken a 'people first' approach to the issue of labelling. By putting 'disabled' upfront they claim solidarity as a group and seek to reclaim a positive identity based on a shared political understanding of their experiences and marginalised status (Oliver, 1992). Disabled people see their situation as one which is imposed from the outside, by society more than by their particular impairment(s). They are critical of the failure to put an end to discrimination in employment, housing, transport and the media, and of patronising attitudes towards them as individuals and as a group. They have identified and analysed pervasive physical and social barriers to their inclusion on equal terms, ranging from lack of access to buildings and public spaces, to inadequate income support, non- or misrepresentation in the media and the structure of service provision and social care agencies. They locate issues around sexuality much more in this social sphere than in relation to specific impairments or to specific sexual 'problems'.

Services for people with learning disabilities have addressed sexual issues in depth (Craft & Craft, 1983; Craft, 1987; Craft, 1994), mainly because some service users are not able to understand enough about sexual behaviour to make their own decisions (Law Commission, 1995). While empowering and educational interventions are preferred in these services, staff and family members sometimes have a more proactive role to play. This is particularly evident in relation to people with severe learning difficulties who, at law, are deemed unable to consent to sexual acts, as they may be to financial transactions or medical interventions (Kaesar, 1992). Many services have explicit policies to guide staff in this area. Such policies usually aim for a balance between supporting people to take informed risks and being clear about the role of staff in providing education/ counselling and protection from abuse.

But while some people with learning disabilities sometimes need staff to act on their behalf, there are no valid arguments for such paternalism towards people with physical or sensory impairments. The fact that they may need practical assistance does not imply that they lack capacity to make their own decisions or to take responsibility for running their own lives. The sexual attitudes which individual staff bring to their roles are, and should remain, secondary to the values of the disabled person her or himself. Staff working with adults are not required to 'agree' with or 'approve' of a specific behaviour, relationship or course of action, merely to define their own boundaries and willingness to provide physical assistance to disabled people in this area of their lives.

Staff working with young disabled people may need to be a bit more parental, but always with a view to what would be acceptable in relation to any other group of young people, depending on their age, culture and maturity. This is not to downplay the ethical or personal complexities of the issues involved, some of which are spelt out in later sections of the report, but to establish autonomy as a first principle from which to approach them. It also underpins the view we take in this report that staff often need disability rights/equality training and training on abuse as a precursor to any specific training on sexuality, otherwise they may interpret this input as a mandate to substitute their own values and judgements for those of the disabled people they serve.

People who use mental health services may fluctuate between these two positions, being at times completely in charge of their own lives and at others in need of support, protection and/or control. Their issues overlap, but are beyond the scope of this report. People with brain injuries may also sometimes need others to intervene on their behalf. There is debate about whether people with chronic or terminal illness should be seen as a distinct group, although their issues also overlap and can be informed by a disability rights perspective. People with Aids are also on the fringes of the disability movement although they face many shared issues. Lois Keith says of this discussion:

Part One Introduction

> *'I understand this concern, but it seems to me that our experiences are on a continuum. We are not either ill or healthy, weak or strong. Some of us are stable and well, others are just acquiring conditions which may be difficult and frightening... I feel there are enough hierarchies created for us from outside... without us creating new hierarchies for ourselves'*
>
> Keith, 1994, p7

We spoke at length about what voice to use in this report. Three of the four authors do not identify themselves as disabled, but the report aimed to encapsulate the views of the core group which consisted entirely of disabled people. We use the term 'we' to include the whole group and 'they' to refer to disabled people and the disability movement.

Part Two
What do disabled people want from services?

The starting position

The *Kama Sutra* describes many sexual positions, but in services for disabled people there seem to be three.

Stop position

The first position forbids sex for disabled people, or places so many barriers in the way that it is effectively not an option for them. Sex might be frowned on in the residential home where a disabled person lives, or only envisaged in circumstances which they cannot create – for example, if they find alternative independent accommodation or manage without personal assistance or other practical resources. This is a way of achieving a 'ban' without saying so.

It might be that sex is forbidden because the service is provided by an agency with a specific set of religious or cultural rules; for example, homosexual acts or extra-marital relationships are disapproved of by many organisations on religious grounds. If the people who use services run by such organisations share a commitment to these views they will not experience them as oppressive. On the other hand, they may not wish to live by these rules but nevertheless they have been 'placed' in this home because it seemed to offer accommodation in the right place or of the right type and with the right level of assistance. Their local authority or other agency may be funding their placement and, even if this body has an overarching equal opportunities policy or statement, it may not challenge the rules as part of the process of drawing up the service agreement or the contract for the individual placement. Gay or lesbian residents may not want to move, or they may not have other options when it comes to their living arrangements, so they may effectively be barred from sexual expression of their choice in their own homes. Agencies may be uncomfortably aware that they fund-raise on the basis of an unstated set of assumptions about the lives of disabled people, which disabled people themselves would challenge if they were given the opportunity.

This used to be the most common position in disability services. Now it is in retreat. For ease we will summarise it as the

 explicit disapproval policy, or stop.

Polite position

The second position is much kinder and more respectful. In theory the service is very much in favour of disabled people's rights. It understands the need to give people 'permission' and privacy when it comes to sexual matters. It may have a written policy, and individual staff may be supportive and encouraging. But it may be that staff hold back from giving direct and practical assistance and/or that the service managers do not want to support them in taking on that role. It might be that, in a mainstream service, staff have not had disability awareness training or assistance to explore what would be involved in working with someone with a physical or sensory impairment. It might be that workers will work with the person as they would with any other individual, but not address the specific issues raised by their impairment out of discomfort or embarrassment – a wish not to get things wrong or to be politically incorrect. And when the crunch comes there do not seem to be ways of making difficult decisions; no-one knows who has the last word or how to manage the fall-out if a member of the fundraising committee learns that a resident has visited a prostitute or decided to become a lone parent or made any other controversial decision.

This is the most common position in current UK services. It works as long as no-one makes too many, or the wrong type of, demands, and it works as long as the issues do not become too visible. We could call it the polite position because it is characterised by a tendency to be embarrassed and a reflex to turn away, by a commitment in theory which seems to fade away in practice.

 Polite position: get ready but hold back

Go-ahead position

The third position involves an unconditional commitment. It acknowledges that disabled people are entitled, in the phrase coined by Shakespeare *et al.* (1996, p207), to 'sexual citizenship', and that the role of services will be to support them in making their own decisions, living their own lives and learning from their own mistakes. The shift from 'care' to 'assistance' facilitates such a stance. When controversial issues arise it will be clear that a principled decision involves respect for the person's autonomy as long as the welfare of others is not jeopardised and it will be likely that the disabled person makes decisions for him or herself.

This position will involve providing just that amount of support which is asked for and needed at the right time and in an unobtrusive way. For some people all it might take is the removal of barriers, while for others it might involve intimate support and physical help. The help will be provided by someone who knew this was to be a part of their job and understood why their input is needed. They would have the necessary maturity and professionalism to be able to give help without its intruding into their own lives and without intruding into the life of the disabled person. It is hard to see how such help could be given without explicit negotiation and a degree of sensitivity in the way the boundaries are crossed and re-established from day-to-day and moment-to-moment. This is a skilled task for both parties in the working relationship. There is always the risk of exploiting or of being exploited, of voyeurism or prurience. The service, or an individual disabled person who is employing their own personal assistants, would need to support staff in finding and maintaining the right balance.

The support needed by the disabled person may not involve direct help but advocacy, counselling or clear information. This would be provided in a way that recognises that people (both service users and staff) are starting from a stationary position and have often had the brakes on for too long. Hence it will be important to provide or facilitate access to other disabled people and their networks, to ensure that individuals have role models to inspire and encourage them as they start out.

 We could call this the 'go-ahead' position because it involves being proactive, taking the initiative, and allowing disabled people to be in the driving seat in their own lives.

Quality indicators in a 'go-ahead' service

The core group worked to develop a set of criteria that could be applied across a range of services and settings. They drew on an analysis of their own experiences of using and providing services. They were in broad agreement about the kinds of support needed to underpin this 'sexual citizenship' (Shakespeare et al., 1996, p207) and how these should be provided.

The core group were particularly concerned with the extent to which services enabled disabled people to stay in control of their own personal space and agendas. The group identified a set of quality indicators which are indicative of this commitment to personal choice and control and which could be applied across these services. The indicators clustered around six key issues. **The six Rs are**:

1 **a rights perspective**: respect for disabled people's sexual rights, options and identities

2 **role models** to inspire disabled people and challenge society's view that disabled people are not sexual

3 user-defined and user-led services which make it possible for disabled people to exercise **responsibility within services** and retain control within service partnerships

4 inclusiveness in a **range of services** with access to places and information guaranteed

5 staff **roles which emphasise assistance** rather than 'care' or 'control', and which rest on appropriate recruitment, training and support, within clear contracts, and on an explicit values base

6 **review and openness**, achieved through listening and learning from internal and external feedback.

Part Two What do disabled people want from services?

These issues are all reflected in the indicators that are reproduced on pages 15–21 in the form of a charter, which you may photocopy to use in your own service.

Supporting the Sexual Rights of Disabled People: Quality Indicators

The six Rs

1. A **rights perspective**: respect for disabled people's sexual rights, options and identities

2. **Role models** to inspire disabled people and challenge society's view that disabled people are not sexual

3. User-defined and user-led services which make it possible for disabled people to exercise **responsibility within services** and retain control within service partnerships

4. Inclusiveness in a **range of services** with access guaranteed to places and information

5. Staff **roles which emphasise assistance** rather than 'care' or 'control', and which rest on appropriate recruitment, training and support, within clear contracts, and an explicit values base

6. **Review and openness** achieved through listening and learning from internal and external feedback

1. A Rights perspective: respect for disabled people's sexual rights, options and identities based on:

- a commitment to sexual rights as a civil liberties issue

- a social model of disability which locates barriers in society rather than in an individual's impairment

- a social model of sexuality which respects identity and choice within a social and political context

- an appreciation of the risks of infantilising, patronising and paternalistic approaches to service provision

- explicitness in policies and contracts

- visibility of disabled people as sexual beings through positive and challenging imagery

- anti-discriminatory practice in relation to disability, gender, ethnicity, culture, class, religion, sexuality, sexual orientation, age and religion.

2. Role models to inspire disabled people and challenge society's view that disabled people are not sexual, including:

- facilitating access to disability arts organisations and publications

- bringing disabled activists into training programmes and educational campaigns

- featuring disabled people from Black and ethnic minority communities in imagery and materials

- involving disabled adults in sex education programmes for disabled young people but also in mainstream settings to counter prejudice

- paying particular attention to the needs for gay and lesbian young disabled people to meet adults who can support them

- displaying challenging and beautiful pictures of disabled people which counter narrow views of beauty or normality

- featuring disabled parents in materials for disabled young people and in ante-natal classes.

3. User-defined and user-led services that make it possible for disabled people to exercise responsibility within services and retain control in service partnerships, evidenced by:

- significant representation of disabled people on management committees and planning, policy and decision-making groups

- employment of disabled people as staff/ volunteers

- evidence of improvement as a result of user comments

- involvement of individual service users in all aspects of recruitment including personnel policies, defining the model of service delivery, prioritising staff activities and drawing up person specifications and job descriptions

- policies which provide continuity of personnel and service provision.

4. Inclusiveness across a range of services with access guaranteed to places and information, including:

- physical accessibility of premises

- appropriate location and transport

- reasonable waiting lists and periods between appointments

- acceptable and aesthetic environment (furnishings, posters, atmosphere, heating, comfort)

- ease of contact (use signing, Minicom, internet, audio, Braille, large print, etc)

- reasonable cost of service and accessibility of funding tailored to individual circumstances

- privacy in residential and other service settings, including choice of single or double rooms, private spaces in day centres, appropriate bathrooms, sound-proof treatment and counselling spaces.

© Pavilion Publishing/Joseph Rowntree Foundation, 2000

5. Staff roles which emphasise assistance rather than 'care' or 'control', and which rest on appropriate recruitment, training and support, within clear contracts, and on an explicit values base, including:

- involvement of disabled people in recruitment and selection

- appropriately qualified, accredited and remunerated staff

- clear job descriptions setting out the nature of the work and areas of intimate care to be undertaken

- equal opportunities in recruitment and employment rights

- commitment to training on disability rights and sexuality for all staff and volunteers

- regular support and supervision from management and professionals

- avenues for making or reviewing difficult decisions or situations in which the worker feels uncomfortable or embarrassed.

6. Review and openness achieved through listening and learning from internal and external feedback, including:

- appropriate record-keeping and adherence to professional codes of conduct

- confidentiality and data protection within stated protocols

- an open and publicised complaints procedure

- regular review of care programmes and individual requirements

- monitoring of service activity, usage and outcomes

- plans to redress service deficiencies at local, regional and national level.

Current service responses

All services have a responsibility to think through how their provision helps or hinders disabled people in their sexual lives. This responsibility extends across administrative boundaries to include agencies which are mainstream as well as those which are targeted specifically at disabled people. It should be exercised whether the agencies provide interventions specifically in relation to sexuality or more general assistance/ support.

Disabled people rely on this network of interconnected services, which include:

- generic services such as the NHS and education, which provide services to all citizens including disabled people and have a generalised bearing on sexuality; the issue might be the accessibility and sensitivity of GP services or the quality and inclusiveness of school sex education programmes

- generic sexuality services – those which provide mainstream services which are specifically related to sexuality or relationship issues such as ante-natal classes, family planning services or Relate

- general disability services, which provide day-to-day support such as housing or residential care or input during the day, personal assistance or home help: in other words, services which have an impact on relationships and sexuality options but in which these issues are a small part of a much broader remit

- specialist sexuality and disability services which provide support to disabled people in the area of sexuality and relationships; for example, advice and information, counselling, infertility treatment or other sexually related services.

The core group, and disabled people in their networks, had experience across this spectrum of services. Although integration within mainstream services is an accepted guiding principle, we found that disabled people were largely invisible to, and within, these generic services. This was signalled by failure to address issues of access and participation and failure to recruit disabled people as workers or volunteers or to target them as potential consumers.

Failure to address disability issues in services which are specifically related to sexuality, such as family planning, HIV, infertility and ante-natal classes, perpetuates the myth among non-disabled people and service organisations that disabled people are not concerned about sexually related issues. It makes reports such as this necessary, not because disabled people want additional services, but because they want to be assured of equal access to ordinary services as members of their communities and not on account of their disability *per se.* Heather Francis (a Black disabled activist) refutes the idea of 'special needs' and says:

> *'disabled people have the same needs as non-disabled people: the only difference is that disabled people's needs are not met'* (1997).

But progress is also needed within disability-related agencies, whether they provide more general support services such as residential or day care, personal assistance and home help, or address sexual issues such as relationship counselling, helpline services and staff training.

Services for disabled people are also located in different sectors, ranging from the large statutory health and social services departments which act as commissioners and care planners, through to provider agencies in the private sector, the larger, more traditional and 'charity-based' disability organisations and those newer voluntary organisations which provide more local services and networks. Moreover, voluntary agencies are changing as they become more involved in direct contracting to provide services, rather than in campaigning around the quality of statutory provision. Their role as providers frequently cuts across their independence as advocates and commentators.

These services are run either by, with or for disabled people. They may address sexuality issues directly with disabled people or indirectly with workers and professionals. But it is the role of disabled people within these agencies that most affects their capacity to offer sensitive and relevant support around sexuality issues. Important messages are signalled by the absence of disabled people on staff or management groups, inaccessible premises and invisibility in promotional material and corporate image, and these in themselves make it impossible to deliver a respectful service. Appropriate values, user involvement, inclusive facilities, ethical fundraising and sensitive feedback are integral to appropriate service provision. So the involvement of disabled people in the planning, running and monitoring of services is critical if attitudes towards sexuality and relationships are to be challenged.

Disabled people are also very alert to the risk of cut-backs in services and to the pressure which assessments and means-testing exert when they are tied to the risk of losing much-needed income. 'Review' may not feel like a positive process if the fear is that it is being approached as a way of saving money. Changes in the rules about practical assistance may seem outside the scope of this report, but one of the core group explained how it feels to be told suddenly that you can only have a bath once a week or that you are no longer eligible for help with cleaning your home. She described how demoralising it was to have to switch from a 'can-do' to a 'can't manage' frame of mind in order to secure a basic income and funding for practical support. And, as this report makes clear, sexuality is an issue which cannot be divorced from wider issues of self-esteem and self-image: these battles leave scars.

Being clear about who is in charge

Sexual issues are less problematic in well-defined situations such as counselling or advice-giving, where the usual boundaries of intimacy are not crossed. In other settings the offering of assistance involves respecting personal space but also being willing to cross personal boundaries in order to facilitate sexual acts. For many disabled people, communal residential settings are a service not of choice but of necessity. As one member of the group said:

> *'I chose to go into residential care… it is just that it was the only choice there was…'*

Once in residential care, maintaining privacy is a constant struggle, whether in relation to staff and their surveillance, or to the realities of communal living with other disabled people. When power is unequally held by staff as opposed to residents, much-needed assistance may be withheld as staff reserve the right to approve or disapprove of residents' sexual relationships, orientation or behaviour.

Cutting the knot between personal assistance and approval relocates responsibility with disabled people and redefines the staff role as one of support rather than of managing

> 'The lack of privacy was an issue. All your life was public knowledge. I was badly resented by staff – care and domestic staff had expectations that I should do my own cleaning but there was a double message which undermined me: they said you can't stay here but you won't manage in the community.' (Member of the core group who married while in residential care)

> 'If someone taps you on the shoulder it shows you're public property. In residential care you're always in public space.'

the disabled person's life. Staff then have to decide their own boundaries and negotiate these as part of their willingness to take up this role. For example, staff would not usually expect to have the latitude to opt out of the responsibility for assisting disabled people with toileting or washing, but they may claim immunity from assisting a couple in getting ready to have sex, or they may not wish to witness specific acts such as masturbation or same-sex relationships. Their withdrawal from these tasks is sometimes legitimated on the grounds of disapproval or protectionism. Differences of opinion about sexual practices or orientation or about observance of religious or cultural teaching are not valid reasons for assistance to be withdrawn, but they may be legitimate grounds on which individual staff could expect clarification about the terms of their employment.

Lack of clarity about the assistance to be given, although it may come across as a power play, often originates in the discomfort of individual staff and the failure to locate these tasks as a legitimate part of their role. The challenge for residential services is to redress this balance and to convey to both existing and potential staff the exact nature of the assistance to be given, allowing space for individuals to accommodate the challenge this presents to their personal values and boundaries. There are occasionally legitimate areas of concern, for example when unequal power may have negated consent on the part of one party and/or given rise to exploitation of another, but these should be regarded as exceptions not rules.

These tensions have to some extent fuelled the independent living movement and motivated many disabled people to employ and direct their own staff, thereby overturning the power relationship between staff and resident most commonly found in residential settings (Zarb & Nadash, 1994; Doyle, 1995). In this situation the power dynamic is overturned, but the issue of boundary negotiation remains, and is often not dealt with sensitively or explicitly in interviews and induction.

Intimate care, whether physical or sexual, inevitably oversteps people's usual boundaries. It moves the relationship between the disabled person and their assistant beyond a normal social or employee relationship and necessitates breaking the usual rules about how to behave, so that intimate tasks can be attended to. Disabled people are usually the experts in managing this dynamic, and it has long been acknowledged that it is they who accumulate skills in putting their assistants at ease and giving precise directions (Davis, 1964), but as Shakespeare *et al.* (1996, p37) remark:

> *'assistance that goes beyond the mundane, such as assistance with sexual activity, has to be negotiated without ground rules or guidance... disabled people who want to employ personal assistants who will facilitate their sexual needs find themselves with no-one to turn to for advice'.*

Members of the core group were also alert to the risk of exploitation of assistants, particularly when those assistants were employed by agencies, and/or were low-paid or badly supported. Whether in residential care or in the person's own home, this is a relationship which requires very skilled negotiation and respect.

User involvement

Despite rhetoric about consultation and partnership, service users still risk being marginalised within the services that exist to serve them. The generic agencies dealing with relationship and sexuality issues which we contacted for this study had not, on the whole, taken steps to initiate or underpin strong links with disabled people and their networks, jeopardising the development of sensitive in-house services and/or onward referrals. Within disability services, and particularly the large paternalistic charities, there were also major issues about control and participation by disabled people and their networks. Some of these service provider agencies are 'federal' in structure, and local branches are under the control of local groups and/ or individuals. Failures of accountability and resistance to change occur in such structures. Others have begun to recognise the importance of including disabled people on management and advisory bodies and staff recruitment and complaints panels, and of underpinning such arrangements to ensure that this commitment is not lost as individuals move on.

User involvement takes different forms and can take place at different levels (Watt, 1997). Winkler (1987, p3) identified six strategies which needed to be in place to make professional services more equal:

1   independent information on service delivery and availability
2   advocacy for patients
3   clinical audits, peer reviews and evaluations made available to user groups
4   effective and independent complaints procedures
5   participation in decision-making
6   collective accountability of user representatives and support for user groups to avoid representatives feeling isolated in their dealings with more powerful interest groups.

Organisations of disabled people, such as the Spinal Injuries Association, have embedded user control within their constitution, which assures that disabled people have the major voice in the running of their affairs. This does turn the tables. For example, a handbook for members of SIA, written by and for disabled people, features an advertisement for specialised fertility treatment, which is a far cry from the notion of professionals giving 'permission' for disabled people to be sexual: it shows disabled people firmly in charge of their sexual and reproductive health choices.

Services for disabled people, in whatever sector, have to attend to a number of functions and networks. They need to ensure clear lines of accountability and governance, whether through traditional line-management structures or through management/trustee committees. They also need to develop a clear picture of their constituencies, and decide whether to work directly with disabled people or via the staff, agencies and professionals who work with them. Either choice is viable, but if both are undertaken they may need to be tackled very differently. Agencies working in this arena also need to locate and access a body to provide ethical input when difficult decisions have to be made, a 'conscience', which, we would argue, should draw heavily on local disability networks.

A barrier often voiced in this respect is that users who attend and participate in such arrangements are atypical and/or unrepresentative. This objection is best resolved by investing in strong and permanent partnership arrangements with disabled people's organisations and networks. This is very significant when it comes to sensitive and power-ridden issues like sexuality. For whose morality is to be the guide in this arena, if not that which is newly emerging within the disability movement?

Part Three
Why are these things important to disabled people?

In this section we set out some of the background thinking which has informed disabled people's priorities in relation to their sexuality. We have drawn on the analysis of the core group and on ideas developed in the literature on disability and on sexuality. Central to these are a 'social' as opposed to bio-medical understanding of disability and of sexuality and a commitment to user involvement in designing and managing services.

This section will be of interest to you if you are interested in the ideas behind changing attitudes and values. If you are more interested in practical matters turn to **Part Four** on page 51 where you can see how services are responding to the challenge of change and find some useful tools for helping you to introduce new ways of relating to disabled people who use your services.

A rights perspective

The most important message the core group wanted to get across in this report is that disabled people are sexual. That is not a difficult idea; what is more difficult to understand is how and why services have made and perpetuated the assumption that they are not.

Until very recently all discussion about sexuality and disability was couched in medical terms. It was all to do with what worked, how to get it or keep it working and with what disabled people with various impairments couldn't do in a 'normal' way. But attitudes towards disability have undergone a sea change in the last thirty years, allowing disabled people to challenge the way their sexual issues are approached as well. The focus has shifted away from individual impairment and 'problems' to throw the spotlight on society's reactions and interactions with disabled people. This means critically exploring what is wrong with a society which marginalises people who are different and oppresses many people by recycling rigid ideas about what is right, beautiful and sexy.

What is 'disability' anyway?

Disabled people have developed an analysis of disability that emphasises society's role in disabling them. Disabled people discriminate between impairment and 'disability', locating disabling barriers in the social and material environment rather than considering them inevitable consequences of particular impairments (Oliver, 1990). They argue that disabled people are as likely to be disadvantaged on account of unemployment, poor housing, inaccessible public transport and buildings, poverty, prejudice and inappropriate service provision as they are by their physical limitations. This analysis confronts the characterisation of disabled people as tragic individuals to be helped, cured or rescued.

If you stop to consider what it is that prevents disabled people from doing the things they want to do, you start to think about questions such as 'what is normal?' and 'who are things designed for?' For example, what prevents someone going to see a film – the fact that they use a wheelchair or the fact that the local cinema has steps and no lift? The changes disabled people want to see are 'the removal of barriers to leading full and active lives, not changes in their physical difference' (Shakespeare *et al.*, 1996, p184).

These barriers are not only concrete and physical, but also part of the way people think and are 'constructed' in their everyday interactions. Disability theorists point out how an artificial line is drawn between those who are normal and those who are 'disabled'. Non-disabled people, says Stone (1995), work very hard to hide their imperfections, for example by straightening their teeth, wearing contact lenses, having their hair dyed or dieting. By working so hard to be seen as 'normal', non-disabled people make disabled people seem more different than they are. Feminist writers have developed a similar line of argument in response to the portrayal of young thin women as the norm, because this pressurises other women to try to fit into the ideal despite their real shapes and sizes and invites them to feel bad if they can't maintain this illusion.

Being seen as, and having role models was defined as a key issue by the core group. Corbett (1994, p355) cited a young woman who says:

> *'If you're growing up disabled or lesbian or gay, you've never seen people like you in magazines or newspapers or on film.'*

Part Three Why are these things important to disabled people?

Things are improving, as one man explained:

> **'For me there were no role models after injury – it was like death... now there's imagery of young tattooed basketball players (wheelchair users). Also I wasn't a 'man' when a fracas occurred in the pub... I was left on the sidelines like the piano player in a Western – neutered. For me there was no engagement with my community. I mean, I was a Sun reader!'**

Disabled people with 'invisible' impairments exercise a degree of personal choice in the extent to which they identify themselves with disabled people and their issues (see Hevey, 1992, who describes his decision to define himself as disabled on account of epilepsy). For example, people who are hard of hearing may pretend not to have missed things other people have said. They may conceal or play down their impairments to 'pass' (Goffman, 1961) – that is, to avoid being seen as part of a devalued group with all the tension and frustration this involves.

Shakespeare *et al.* (1996) suggested that challenging this normal/abnormal split by 'challenging notions of beauty and normality' could help everyone, not only disabled people, because it

> *'has the potential to release others from the tyranny of our contemporary obsession with health, fitness and good looks'.*

Disabled people also find themselves judged and taken in by these (impossible) standards, and even apply them to other disabled people. They are judged by each other as well as by non-disabled people against these pervasive images of normality. For example, Shakespeare *et al.* (1996, p49) quoted a disabled person who challenged the

> *'real hierarchy of what is acceptable appearance within the disabled community: what is beautiful? what is ugly? At the top is someone who sits in a wheelchair but looks perfect. I have a friend who has cerebral palsy; she always says cerebral palsy is the dregs. They drool and have a speech impairment, movement problems, that kind of thing. On the high end of the scale is the person with a polio disability, because physically they look okay. It is something we need to work on'.*

That is why disabled people see it as so important to reject these negative values and put positive ones in their place.

Disabled artists and film-makers have begun to do this by flouting the stereotyped way in which disabled people are usually portrayed (Hevey, 1997; Lapper, 1997). Increasingly we see disabled people in fashion and sports photography, in painting and sculpture. Hughes & Paterson (1997) comment on the

> *'extent to which impairment can be... reconstructed in terms of pride and positivity as opposed to a site for the existential fears of the non-disabled community'* (p332).

It is as if images can be reclaimed in the same way as language/labels and made to work for disabled people rather than against them.

Part Three Why are these things important to disabled people?

And what is 'sex'?

The same sort of thing happens around sex. Everyone imagines there is a normal way of doing it or having it, because this is what we see on the TV screen or on page 3. Everyone talks about how much rather than how little sex they have and no-one talks about the doubts, fumblings and misunderstandings. They may appeal to narrow medical or 'evolutionary' explanations about why men and women behave the way they do, without considering the extent to which social roles, attitudes and opportunities shape our options and desires. Gay men and lesbians have only very recently been able to acknowledge their different sexuality. And it was only when *Viagra* came on the market as a possible 'cure' that many men felt able to acknowledge that they sometimes had problems with their sexual 'performance'. Their experience is a very clear example of how people hide difficulties in order to 'pass' as normal. Normality only survives as an ideal because people feel afraid to 'come out' and be open about who they really are.

So it would be a mistake to assume that there is such a thing as 'normal' sexuality for disabled people to aspire to or that what is normal is necessarily good. One disabled woman challenged the myth that 'normal' people enjoy unlimited sexual pleasure:

> '*I see my limitations only as parameters… if you are a sexually active disabled person, and comfortable with the sexual side of your life, it is remarkable how dull and unimaginative non-disabled people's sex lives can appear. I am often left feeling surprised and smug when I hear my non-disabled friends bemoan the stale approaches of lovers, the tedium of flopping into the same sexual position, the lack of open and honest communication.*' Shakespeare *et al.*, 1996, p203

Moreover, sexualities vary depending on all kinds of experiences, values and situations and only a narrow range get reflected back to us as 'normal'. Sexualities are just as much shaped by life in hospitals, special schools or residential care as they are by public schools, the nightclub scene or the local church, synagogue or mosque. Individuals have more or less choice and control in relation to all these influences.

'Coming out' and acknowledging differences

When people acknowledge shared differences they can stop being afraid of not being normal. This is a similar process if you are a disabled person or if you are gay or lesbian. Corbett (1994, p393) describes 'coming out' as gay or lesbian as a journey towards being 'proudly visible'. Shakespeare et al. (1996, p58) summarises 'coming out' as disabled as:

> *'redefining disability as a political oppression, identifying collectively with other disabled people and with disability culture: overcoming internalised oppression… it therefore has personal and psychological benefits as well as social and political value'.*

Survivors of sexual and other abuses also use this phrase to describe a transition from hiding what has happened to them towards acknowledgement, healing and empowerment.

Young disabled people are often not helped to be upfront about their disability and to make links with other disabled people. Disability issues are not included within the national curriculum and, if referred to at all, come within the crowded personal, social and vocational agenda. The disability movement and its ideas are usually missing. For example, young deaf students to whom we spoke were not aware of debates about whether their community should be allied with the disabled community or seen as a linguistic and cultural minority. They may be taught the literature and history of many countries and communities but not their own (Young *et al.*, 1998). This absence matters as much in mainstream schools as it does in special schools, because non-disabled people are also not learning how to interact respectfully with their disabled peers or having their views about disabled people challenged.

When disabled people feel confident, as they do when they are supported by involvement with other disabled people, they are freer to explore what sexuality works for them rather than waste their energy trying to pretend to be like everyone else (or at least how everyone else is trying to pretend to be). Longmore (1987, p73) summed this up when he said that:

> *'ultimately disabled people enter relationships out of the strength of their own identities as persons with disabilities'.*

Personal as well as social issues

But seeing the world like this doesn't mean that disabled people do not have specific issues or feelings about their own situations, impairments or opportunities. Pretending everything is fine may actually reinforce the status quo.

So-called normal people not only hide behind their appearance, but they also 'disguise' any pain, illness and other limitations in order to appear normal (Stone, 1995, p420). This makes it seem as if disabled people are the only people with vulnerabilities, which allows 'non-disabled people' to start treating disabled people as 'other', for example by feeling sorry for them, or wondering how they manage their sex lives. Several writers have developed this theme, pointing to the way so-called 'normal people' project their fears and vulnerabilities on to anyone with a visible disability (Finkelstein, 1997; Oliver, 1990). Hevey (1992) says that disabled people are like 'dustbins' for all those imperfections and fears which no-one else wants to face up to.

Disabled people have argued that a model which replaces the projections and pity of others with a self-imposed kind of 'stiff upper lip' is unhelpful and unnecessarily restrictive. Lois Keith (1994, p7) agrees with the need to counter the popular view of ourselves as 'sick, tragic figures', but warns that if we do this

> *'by denying the realities of our lives, which are sometimes painful and sad, we are just swapping the "tragic and brave" model the world is so fond of for another kind of dangerous myth in which we must always be fighters. Apart from anything else, this is a very male way to look at the world'.*

This issue is reflected in debates among non-disabled women about how far they can dare to 'go public' in relation to female maladies such as period pains, pregnancy and menopausal symptoms without jeopardising their struggle for equality. Some disabled people, especially disabled feminists (Morris, 1991), have argued that hiding vulnerability and/or glossing over the negative impact of impairment colludes with oppression rather than challenges it.

Overcoming the legacy of institutional attitudes

Some professionals see their role as giving disabled people 'permission' to be sexual, but if permission has been needed in the past it is largely to compensate for damaging experiences in which people have been shamed, taunted or excluded when they have expressed their sexuality. Older members of the group had experienced blanket disapproval of sexuality and relationships as one facet of the damaging legacy of institutional care. They described losses and separations in childhood: the constant scrutiny of relationships, lack of privacy or personal space and a requirement to live by other people's religious beliefs. The disapproval included taboos against all forms of sexual activity, whether masturbation, heterosexual sex in or out of marriage, same-sex relationships or parenthood.

Some of the core group had horror stories about their own childhoods in segregated institutions where emotional ties were broken and sex forbidden. The core group had innumerable stories about the disapproval and taboos they faced whenever they tried to form relationships or express their sexuality. One group member described how a friend was dealt with when he removed himself to his room to masturbate:

> 'He had a room of his own. Because I hadn't been in the institution very long so I didn't have a room of my own, and he disappeared as he usually did, and I didn't think any more of it. Suddenly I heard this sort of forbidden shout, you know, "How dare you do that" and this carer... member of staff, got a bucket of cold water and actually chucked it over him because he was doing his own thing and I always remember that, I was so shocked – not for the fact he was doing what he was doing – that didn't bother me because he was in his own room – you know, he was free to do what he wants or he should be – but it was the fact that the member of staff thought they had the right to chuck a bucket of water over him'.

The literature and the experience of the group also confirmed the risk of sexual abuse, particularly for deaf young people in institutional environments.

The need for help is still often used to disqualify disabled people from sexual activity or relationships. To qualify for marriage, disabled people in the past had to earn their way out of residential care; if they were going to claim the right to be sexual, they had to give up their entitlement to assistance. When one member of the core group married while living in residential care, she and her husband faced daily resistance and hostility; cleaners refused to clean their rooms (arranged now as a bedroom and sitting room instead of two single rooms) as if two people living together made more mess than those same people living in adjacent rooms.

Independence, as opposed to autonomy, remains the explicit goal of many services. Inability to perform trivial tasks was seized upon as a justification for imposing rules or moral judgements. One core group member said he would much rather go to work in his job at the Citizen's Advice Bureau than spend hours putting on his socks! Most people do not regard washing up as a test that they have to pass before becoming sexually active! Nevertheless, a need for physical help is still often used as an excuse for denying sexuality or limiting sexual expression, not only in institutional but also in family/informal settings.

Working to prevent these negative experiences will enable disabled people to stay in charge of their own sex lives and ask for, rather than have to accept, the input of non-disabled people, if and when they require practical assistance.

Different issues as well as common ground

Solidarity should not be confused with uniformity. Disabled people share the experience of living in a disablist and unequal society but little else – they are drawn from all sections of the community, from different religious and ethnic minority groups and varying socio-economic backgrounds. Pfeiffer (1991) found the usual inequalities (according to gender and ethnicity) in employment and income status, and that white disabled men hung on to a privileged position within the disability community. Hanna & Rogovsky (1991) reported that disabled women were less likely to be or to stay married than disabled men, to be well-educated or to be in well-paid employment.

Much of the early disability literature was based on the analysis of white disabled men and reflected their particular perspective. When disabled women started to write independently they had different things to say. Jenny Morris challenged the idea that the experience of disabled men is 'representative of the disabled experience in general' (1993, p85) and pointed out that a concern with 'gender' does not mean just a focus on the specific needs of disabled women but also a clearer look at the issues which face men.

Morris says that if you take a gender-aware approach to the issues faced by disabled men as well as women, you see that disabled men are often in a double bind as

> *'being a man and being disabled are two incongruous roles – in the sense that being a man in our society is to be strong, assertive and independent... the failure to measure up to what is socially defined as being a man can be devastating'.*
> Morris, 1993, p88–89

Certainly a great deal of the more traditional scientific literature about sexuality and disability focuses on male sexual functioning after impairment and on strategies for remediating or replacing erections. Some organisations have tended to endorse this traditional view of male sexual 'performance' in penetrative sex by giving advice on sex aids and treatments rather than suggesting alternatives.

Disabled men have to make choices about how far they try to uphold traditional gender and sex roles, or redefine what it means to be a 'new' man in the light of their experiences of disability. But this may sound glib to anyone being forced to change the way they do things as a result not only of their own impairment but of the responses of potential partners.

Part Three Why are these things important to disabled people?

Morris sees the issues for disabled women in a different light, in that the qualities expected of disabled people are the same but more extreme versions of those which are approved of in women generally. She argues that:

> *'the fact that dependence is a key part of the social construction of gender for women and of the social construction of disability means that women's powerlessness is confirmed by disability'*.
> Morris, 1993, p89

So while disabled men are encouraged to be 'super-men', disabled women may find their sexuality discounted as women as well as on account of their impairment. Members of the core group wondered if this reflects not only an old-fashioned view that women should 'lie back and think of England' but also a taboo about disabled women having children. Disabled women are treated ambivalently: they may face prejudice when they seek to become mothers, but find themselves subject to assumptions about their willingness and/or ability to take on housework or care for existing family members.

Disabled women also share with other women the difficulties of meeting potential partners in a safe environment, and women in the core group voiced their caution about the motives of men (especially non-disabled men) who want to have sex with them (Shakespeare *et al.*, 1996, p96).

> **A certain type of man gravitates towards some disabled women. The issue is not so much about a relationship as about power and control.**

Moreover, disabled women are more likely than disabled men to be excluded from the sexual scene of their choice by the rigid rules which apply to all women because, as Stone argues (1995, p420):

> *'women even more than men are judged, and judge themselves, by their appearance. The dominant culture may teach men to be concerned about their appearance, but it does not teach men that their value as individuals depends upon their ability to disguise their bodies and make them appear to be something other than they actually are'.*

Issues for disabled gay men and lesbians

Gay men and lesbians face other conflicting expectations. They have to contend with discrimination at law and widespread prejudice. One might expect close links between gay and disability movements because their claims for equal treatment are based on similar arguments and analyses of exclusion (Morris, 1993; Corbett, 1994). But disabled gay men and lesbians may be pushed out or silenced in the disability movement on account of being gay and in the gay/lesbian scene on account of being disabled. Gay men in particular may get the 'cold shoulder' even though they might expect their non-disabled peers to make connections:

> *'You would expect people on the gay scene to be the most understanding but they're not. The gay scene is simply horrendous. It all revolves around looks'*
> Corbett, 1994, p344, citing Veskner, 1993

Moreover, individual gay men and lesbians often find their sexuality and their relationships overlooked in the context

Part Three Why are these things important to disabled people?

of their contacts with services. A gay man interviewed for an article on sexuality and social work complained about an assessment of his so-called 'needs' which completely overlooked his sexual relationship.

This individual invisibility may be reflected at a service level, where overt commitment to sexual rights for gay men and lesbians may be played down in the interest of fund-raising or by agencies which have an explicit religious affiliation. For example, SPOD reported having to tone down information on gay sex included in a leaflet on HIV/Aids at

NEEDS 'WENT OVER THEIR HEADS'

Peter Simons (not his real name) first applied for community care services two and a half years ago, when he was living alone after his partner had died. 'During the assessment I didn't feel that my needs as a gay disabled person were being addressed. I didn't feel at all comfortable about having to justify my needs as a gay disabled man.

'The disability stuff was difficult enough, but talking about "cultural appropriateness" went right over their heads', he says. He eventually found someone in social services who was more supportive, though he says it took 'a while'.

He now has a partner who is also disabled and was re-assessed recently.

'I raised the issue of my unmet needs, and they offered me residential care without thinking of the implications. I thought they were taking the piss. I asked them whether they had a place where I could sleep with my partner. I also asked who would assess my partner's needs if he spent the night with me in residential care.' Not

> surprisingly, Simons has stayed in his own home.
>
> Simons' partner also lives in his own home and has not yet felt able to tell social services that he is gay. He says that he would be forced to tell if either of them wanted to make sure that their respective homes were fully accessible to both. 'This all means that you'd have to tell social services who you wanted to have sex with, when and where.'
>
> Transport is another difficulty for them, as is the benefits system. 'If you want to lead a reasonably full life you have to get social services to assess your sexual needs, and to justify your sexual activity, which is horrendously abusive really. So a lot of lesbians and gay men just aren't approaching social services for help', Simons says.
>
> (Reproduced from *Community Care*, 27 March–2 April 1997, p21, with thanks.)

the request of the last government. We were told that another national agency had been told by its governing body that it could not mention S&M or fetishism in its literature, despite their argument that these are valid expressions of sexuality between consenting adults.

Issues for Black disabled people

Disabled people from Black and ethnic minority communities also face conflicts and compromises. This is sometimes referred to as 'double discrimination' but Stewart (1993) argues that

> *'being a Black disabled person is not a "double" experience, but a single one grounded in British racism'.*
> Stewart, 1993, p99

Black communities struggle economically and socially against what is increasingly acknowledged to be institutionalised racism in British society. So Black disabled people face two sets of prejudices and may find themselves in a relatively powerless position in relation to their own communities (as a result of unemployment and lack of access to housing and other resources), as well as in relation to the white community and the predominantly white disability movement.

Moreover

> '...ethnic minority groups can be just as prejudiced towards disabled people as their white neighbours'.
> Stewart, 1993, p98–99

Of course services need to take into account different cultural expectations and customs around personal hygiene, skin care, gender and caring roles (Bignall & Butt, 1999). But this is not enough, as Black disabled people may question these structures, and the position they take for themselves needs to be respected and upheld. One member of the core group made it clear that she had defied her own community and its religious teachings to marry and have children as a disabled woman. Black disabled people may be busy countering limiting assumptions and expectations within their own cultures at the same time as they are struggling to get their needs addressed against a more pervasive backdrop of discrimination. Black disabled people have also challenged their status within the disability movement by setting up their own networks and pressure groups.

Conclusions

In offering this analysis, group members reflected on interlocking areas of discrimination and multi-layered oppression, including poverty, racism, homophobia, unemployment and sexual abuse. They unanimously felt diminished by the invisibility of disabled people in the wider culture and by their absence as role models to reflect a breadth of opportunities for full citizenship and sexual possibilities. This wilful absence was exacerbated for disabled gay men and lesbians and made more complicated for disabled people from Black and ethnic minorities. For disabled parents it carried real and immediate penalties for them and their children, leading to barriers in receiving basic and respectful health and childcare services. The group considered that disability arts are making a hopeful inroad into this vacuum, but there is still a long way to go and many examples of crass stereotypes in the mainstream media.

These barriers are made more acute by lack of information and lack of choice in relation to basic provision such as housing, employment, transport, benefits, health and social care, as well as in relation to more specific input on sexuality and counselling, sexual health and parenting.

It is against this backdrop that sexuality is best understood and approached as a key civil liberties issue for disabled people.

Part Four
Working towards good practice

In this section we will take each of the six clusters of quality indicators and demonstrate how far services are working towards these standards, describing examples of positive practice from a range of service settings.

The fieldwork in this project had a number of aims, including:

- testing out the criteria we had drawn up in a broad sample of services which had been identified by the core group as working towards good practice in their commitment to sexual rights

- identifying how a sexual rights framework could be implemented in both mainstream and specialist services

- offering support within the interview process to those services which were committed to reviewing their practice and policies.

In order to illustrate how current service provision measures against these criteria, we have taken each cluster in turn and looked for indicators that services are working towards good practice in relation to each set of aspirations.

Within many of the services visited, the commitment to a sexual rights perspective was evident, but in other situations it had yet to be translated into practice. This report does not seek to 'point the finger' in any way, and we would like to thank service managers and staff for their openness and honesty in talking about shortfalls in their own services[1]. It is not our intention to expose poor or unimaginative practice, but to identify the positive steps which are being taken to ensure that disabled people can exercise their sexual rights. Where we have mentioned specific services we have done so to illustrate a particular point, but even if you do not see your own service described in detail that does not mean that we did not learn from our broader consultations. We hope the report reflects the excitement we picked up from services that the time is ripe for innovative service development.

A rights perspective

This is about respect for disabled people's sexual rights, options and identities.

A commitment to sexual rights needs to be evident in words, imagery, behaviour and visual presentation. It was most consistently and explicitly found in the specialist counselling agencies we contacted. One service which offers counselling to disabled people around personal relationships and sexuality states clearly in its literature that it aims to

> *'promote the understanding that people with physical disabilities... have a right to a sexual identity which is acknowledged, respected and supported'.*

---

[1] We have not named specific services, in order to protect the anonymity of the people we spoke to, but where an agency has a very specific brief and/or is unique and therefore recognisable we have referred to it directly.

This standpoint is endorsed and expanded in its equal opportunities policy, which also recognises the potential for multiple oppression caused by homophobia:

> *'Someone with a physical disability suffers discrimination because of society's attitude to disability and to sexual identity. If someone has a homosexual identity, this discrimination will be even more extreme.'*

But the literature provided by services offering practical support to disabled people in residential or community settings demonstrated a more watered-down commitment to civil liberties and sexual rights. Although words such as 'choice', 'rights', 'fulfilment', 'independence', 'privacy' and 'dignity' are frequently cited and these concepts could embrace sexual rights, the agencies tend not to be explicit about sexual activity or sexuality within presentational or promotional material. For example, a brochure for potential residents of one care home outlined facilities and activities, with no mention of what is 'accepted' and 'acceptable' behind the closed doors of one's bedroom. In practice, however, there was evidence that these issues are being addressed in appropriate ways, but the larger, more traditional organisations have a long way to go in overturning a patriarchal and often rather puritanical sexual culture in their 'homes'.

Agencies offering services and support to the 'general public' frequently make no reference to disabled people; they act as if this exclusion was in fact inclusion. They may allude to the fact that their premises are accessible to mothers with buggies, but not mention mothers with wheelchairs.

The social model of disability

Lip service (at least) to the social model of disability is standard in non-medicalised services for disabled people. For example:

- The representative of a service working with young disabled people said *'society has a habit of caring for, smothering, nurturing a disabled person as a child, who therefore does not want sex. We try to combat this.'*

- The written aim of another service stated that *'each individual has a responsibility to be accountable for their own health and wellbeing, and not to become a victim as their disability develops. Each person must as far as possible be a full and responsible participant in illness as well as health.'*

However, there were also services in which the social model provided a rubric but was not fully understood or translated into practice, or where ideals had been flagged up but the conflicts arising between different principles not spelt out. For example, confidentiality and consultation may clash, as might the rights of users and parental involvement.

One counselling service made a case for being flexible in its theoretical and practice approach, to respond to the different needs of their clients. A rigid adherence to the social model to the total exclusion of the medical model could jeopardise the counselling process. As one person said:

> *'everyone feels fed up and angry about their disability at some stage and this may come to the fore most in their counselling sessions. As counsellors, we need to be led by the client and where they come from'.*

But as we have seen, it is possible to address issues of impairment without jettisoning the social and collective perspective.

Translating the rights perspective into action

Although the core group were very clear about the principles which underpin practice in this area, no-one was naïve enough to think that they will provide easy answers in complex situations. Many of the interviewees gave examples of how their service translated policy into practice. In so doing they had to navigate a number of barriers without losing sight of individual rights.

A number of issues and dilemmas arose in the context of facilitating sexual relationships and of how explicit this assistance could and should be. Free condoms were available in some settings – but their visibility and accessibility were sometimes restricted. They are of little use if they are in the desk drawer of the manager, who goes off duty at 5pm, a situation which betrays a certain ambivalence! In one agency, a disabled woman and a quadriplegic man spent time together on a daily basis. Ostensibly no questions were asked about what took place 'behind closed doors', although there was an unspoken assumption that the role of the staff was to prepare the couple to conduct a sexual relationship. Staff in another setting acknowledged the existence of sexual relationships, but maintained an unwritten rule (which, it was admitted, was quite illogical) that residents should sleep in their own beds. The provision of single beds also created a practical barrier to 'sleeping together' (except in the rooms adapted for couples, of which we saw few).

In another service for young people, a distinction was made about assisting them on to their own as opposed to their partner's beds; people with impairments which would prevent them getting up on their own were not helped onto their partner's bed, even at their request. The justification for this was that they might later change their mind... However, other students recognised that this unfairly discriminated against more impaired young people, and circumvented the problem by putting their friends on whatever bed they liked, when they were asked. This was a clear example of a situation where the need for physical assistance was being confused with issues of autonomy. There was no reason why people with more severe impairments should be less likely to know what they wanted or be less willing to take chances than other young people; only their physical limitations prevented them from acting on these wishes.

Same-sex relationships are particularly vulnerable to interference or ambivalent support. One service described how two men had formed a relationship in a setting that provided both day and residential care. They claimed this was only an issue because there was an age gap and not because of the nature of the relationship, even though the young man was over the age of consent. The parents of the young man were also thought to be unhappy about the relationship. This required an appropriate and sensitive response by the agency if it was to support the rights of the individual while allaying the anxieties of the parents and helping them to give their son space to make his own decisions.

These examples focus on more institutional settings, but dilemmas are also present for personal assistants, who are in a difficult position when they enter the home of a couple or family and encounter each household's particular 'culture'. Although their first approach is usually to ask the disabled person how they want tasks to be tackled, they also need to be aware that partners or spouses have feelings. We discussed at length the extent to which employment contracts should spell out the extent of, and limits to, the expectations on personal assistants to facilitate sexual acts or relationships.

> ### *Key messages*
>
> 1. **A model of disability and sexuality which focuses on social processes such as expectations, imagery and barriers is more useful than one which dwells on individual impairments and biological differences.**
>
> 2. **Young disabled people should not be disadvantaged in their relationships or compromised in their autonomy. They should be helped to make contact with disabled adults who can help them develop a strong sense of their identity as disabled people.**
>
> 3. **Openness and explicitness, however awkward, should be the goal, so that individual members of staff who make courageous stands in support of disabled people who need assistance are not left unprotected and unsupported. Explicitness also acts to protect disabled people from unwanted sex, while fair and open discussion allows workers to negotiate around any aspects of the work they do not wish to undertake.**

Role models to inspire disabled people and challenge society

The view that needs challenging is that disabled people are not sexual.

This is one area of practice where all services have a distinct choice, because if they are not part of the solution they are very much part of the problem. Services for disabled people which do nothing to counter invisibility or 'victim' images are not just being neutral. Failing to feature disabled people in publicity material cannot be regarded as an acceptable oversight. Displaying images of adult relationships which do not include disabled people undermines the sexual citizenship which disabled people seek and fails to educate non-disabled people into new ways of seeing disabled people.

We did, however, come across some imaginative art being done at a national further education college for disabled and non-disabled students in which disability was the focus of the work. This work allowed disabled young people to see themselves and explore how they wanted to present themselves. Images and a range of media were used to explore these new aesthetics and enable students to explore and express their physical selves. The department drew on the work and input of successful disabled artists and promoted the students' work in the public arena.

Disability arts play a central role in combating the generic invisibility of disabled people in our culture and the more specific lack of sexual role models throughout the media. These range from poetry, rap and rock music, novels and visual arts, theatre, photography, radio and TV, including the work of Channel 4 and the BBC's Disability Programmes

Unit. The increasing visibility of disabled sports, weight training and dance also contributes to this new aesthetic.

> *Key messages*
>
> 1. **Disabled people want to be visible, not airbrushed out of the picture; they want to be re-represented in positive and exciting images. Services and organisations for disabled people should help disabled people present themselves and their bodies in new and challenging ways, express themselves through their bodies, art, photography and other imagery and display their work and ideas in a proactive way.**
>
> 2. **Generic services do not serve disabled people well if they do not portray them as potential consumers of their 'ordinary' services. Inclusive publicity materials would ensure that disabled people are there – visible and taken-for-granted consumers of health and other sexuality services.**
>
> 3. **Disability arts empower disabled people by challenging stereotypes and expressing powerful alternative views. Accessing new means of self-expression and presentation should be an important part of the agenda of services which exist to support disabled people, especially disabled young people.**

Services that enable disabled people to exercise responsibility

User-defined and user-led services can allow disabled people to take responsibility and to retain control within service partnerships.

With few exceptions, disabled people were not well represented on the governing bodies of the agencies serving them, and the proportion of disabled people rarely outweighed non-disabled people on these bodies. One specified in its constitution that 75% of its management committee should be disabled and elected by its membership, which demonstrates that it is possible.

Whilst smaller community-based services for disabled people demonstrate a commitment to expanding this representation, the larger – typically residential – services were less likely to target disabled people as potential governors. This may be due to the philanthropic, often Christian, foundations of these organisations, which have traditionally targeted the fundraising capacities of the 'great and the good' in preference to the personal contributions that can be made by disabled people who have experienced (or escaped from) residential care. (Of course, some of the 'great and the good' are also disabled.) However, there are problems in attracting people to join committees. As one disabled manager said, *'It's not just a question of apathy, some disabled people do not want to spend their life focusing on disability'*. But these barriers had not deterred another group from working towards an all-disabled management committee.

Some alternative structures had been developed to act as a focus for the views of disabled service users, for example:

- One residential home had a residents' representative committee, to which residents were elected annually. The group met on a monthly basis with managers and members of the council of management. This meeting was described as 'positive and influential' by one of the managers.

- A personal assistants service established a clients' forum which meets twice a year. Representation consists of four disabled people, managers from the local social services department, personal assistants, carers and trustees of the agency.

- One day care service has a regular support group, but since 1991 its focus had shifted from being a members' committee with clout, to a fundraising group.

- User involvement in counselling settings is less comfortable because of the need to assure the anonymity of clients. One service had distributed evaluation forms to clients at the close of their first session, but acknowledged that meaningful comments would only be received following the conclusion of the counselling process and a period of reflection.

The employment of disabled people

'I could see no way anyone could set up any kind of service... if there was no consultation or representation of that client group in the workforce. If there is no collegial equality, there is unlikely to be a feeling of respect for the client group, albeit on an unconscious level.'
White, 1996

Commitment to recruiting disabled staff varied according to the nature of the service. While in most circumstances the small specialist agencies were able to attract an acceptable (to them) proportion of disabled people to their staff, other agencies were less attentive to this priority. One national organisation for people with a specific form of impairment has a counselling service run by qualified counsellors who are all disabled. This is advertised to their members. We were disappointed to see that the important life skills that disabled people bring were downgraded in the recruitment process in favour of more traditional competencies, to the advantage of non-disabled applicants. For example, proficiency in sign language was not considered a key competency, even where this was the first language of service users. In other settings, wheelchair access was limited for staff as it was for users. One specialist counselling agency had been successful in recruiting staff and volunteers with different life experience and different personal characteristics, although it regretted the problems in identifying and recruiting counsellors with sensory impairments who would have provided an additional and important resource for clients with sensory impairments.

The involvement of disabled people in the recruiting process might ensure that disabled applicants are not discriminated against and that their qualities and life experiences are appropriately valued. This had become the norm in personal assistants schemes, but not in the residential and day services we visited. Where service users were involved in recruitment it was important that this was not tokenistic; disabled people should be involved in all stages of the process, from drawing up advertisements and job descriptions to sitting as equals on interview panels and appointment boards[1].

---

[1] Townsley *et al.* (1997) address a similar set of issues in relation to people with learning disabilities.

Key messages

1. Users should be involved in the design and governance of services wherever possible, and particularly in those aspects of service which impact upon the freedoms of disabled people in their personal and sexual relationships. To this end, disability equality training (which also addresses sexual rights) should be available on a regular basis for mainstream organisations, planners and commissioners and non-disabled management committees.

2. Agencies serving disabled people need to employ disabled people throughout their organisations and particularly in roles which directly support disabled people in their emotional and sexual lives. Role models and life experience are important alongside more orthodox qualifications. Training for disabled people to assume these roles should be developed and funded.

3. Disabled people who are elected to management committees or as members of staff should be accorded equal status and assured an equal say in decision-making bodies and staff teams.

Inclusiveness across a range of services

This should include guaranteed access to places and information.

'Choice' and 'integration' are meaningless slogans if premises are not accessible to disabled people, but many services, particularly those which are offered to the general public, are not equipped with ramps, stairlifts or loop systems to accommodate different needs. This betrays a lack of inclusion and discriminatory expectations. As one disabled student remarked:

> *'we'll know things have changed if they ever get round to putting condoms, tampons and mirrors in disabled loos!'*

Family planning, ante-natal services and relationship counselling services are all routinely offered in places which are inaccessible to disabled people. Even where a base-line had been reached, there were questions about whether adaptations had gone far enough. For example, a service might have provided a ramp to the front door but then restrict wheelchair users to the ground floor. Services we visited which were specifically designed for disabled people had demonstrated considerable ingenuity in acquiring fully accessible premises, even though this had often only been achieved through persistent investigation of the possibilities.

Some seemingly suitable premises had been rejected because they gave out the wrong 'message'. For example, a specialist counselling service preferred not to use the facilities within a day centre as they thought this might cut across the possibility of real choice that the individual has made to use the service:

> *'It's 2 o'clock, so it's time for the physio.*
> *It's 4 o'clock, so it's time for the counsellor!'*

Counselling at home was not favoured for the same reasons, but was offered to disabled people who were confined to the home and genuinely not able to access transport.

In some cases, compromises have to be made, for example where it is necessary to balance wheelchair accessibility with good local transport facilities. Premises we visited also varied from the purpose-built and well-decorated to the shabby and institutionalised. Long corridors are daunting and off-putting to people with minimal mobility. Drab old-style canteens and refreshment areas, peeling green paint and smelly toilets are depressing, but we did see them on our visits. We also saw some buildings which managed to incorporate high-tech solutions to practical problems with a high standard of aesthetics and comfort.

Art by disabled people, challenging imagery and bright/light colours were possible, alongside functional adaptations such as good lighting, clear signs and defined edges. Even where smaller agencies were struggling to overcome the limitations of necessarily low-cost premises, there were small things which they could have, and yet had not, tackled. So, for example, in one service training events took place in a downstairs room with no pictures on the wall, when positive images of disabled people in a variety of roles or relationships might have challenged the low status attached to disabled people's services and to issues of sexuality within them.

Generic agencies seemed to have demonstrated the least commitment to accessibility and location. For example, one national organisation with a federal structure of local bodies 'encourages' the use of accessible buildings, but no penalties are exacted if this is not achieved or prioritised. Of course, this restricts accessibility and usage by disabled people, not only as clients but also as staff members, volunteers and management committee members.

Premises were particularly important in relation to residential (and day) settings, where privacy and room lay-out could cut across well-meaning platitudes. Disabled people often have no access to suitable places where personal or sexual relationships can flourish, especially if they are living in residential care or in their parents' homes.

The design of residential settings often reflects decisions to opt for spacious communal areas (requiring minimal supervision by staff) to the detriment of private space. Bedrooms are often small and single and rarely have double beds. But there were thoughtful exceptions. One residential unit for young disabled people (aged 16 to 30) was designed so that bedrooms were roomy enough to accommodate two large wheelchairs (although the beds were still single!)

Accommodation for couples is almost non-existent. Staff of another residential home recognised that the single bedrooms in their establishment were not conducive to creating a 'romantic' atmosphere, and supported the use of alternative venues, including the day centre (outside 'opening hours') and the grounds, but they recognised that this was hardly satisfactory.

The availability of the services

Take-up of services depends on their availability at a location and within a timeframe that is acceptable to the client. We have already discussed the limitations of existing services in terms of accessibility and acceptability. But there is also an issue about how people get to know about services which are available and whether they can access them directly or have to be referred through other agencies. SPOD has a role as a national clearing house for enquiries. Another specialist counselling service reported that it frequently receives phone calls from individuals all over Britain who enquire (in vain) whether similar services exist in their own area.

> **'There is very little therapy for disabled people by disabled people…only two in London…there are some non-disabled therapists but they don't know about the social model.'**

Waiting times may also act as a barrier. A generic counselling service regularly has a waiting time of over three weeks for an assessment, followed by a similar wait for the first appointment. Another specialist counselling service we visited (DISCERN) managed to work with no waiting list itself, but where it refers clients on to the local NHS psychotherapy service, there is a waiting time of two to three years.

SPOD provides a telephone counselling and advice service for three sessions each week. It refers people on for longer-term counselling or to other agencies where this is wanted, but in 70% of cases callers ask for specific information. It is not clear from the figures at what point people require information: whether their call is a first port of call which they will follow up when they have absorbed the information they have received, or a last resort when other sources of support and information have failed them.

Access to information about sex and sexuality

It is not only premises which need to be accessible. Disabled people are also denied choice because information is not accessible or made available to them. Literature produced by both specialist and generic agencies rarely makes reference to the availability of a Minicom system; they tend to publish leaflets in one size of print format, often reproduced on background colours which reduce visibility. On the other hand it is encouraging that some material is now being addressed directly to disabled people rather than filtered via professionals and/or parents, however inexpertly it is being done. Developments in IT and access to the Internet may make some of these obstacles obsolete.

Training courses and packs on sexuality and disability have been developed in recent years. The majority of them target professionals as their audience, and few have been designed specifically by or for disabled people to promote sexuality within a civil liberties perspective and/or to bring this message home to a wider audience.

One of the most worrying issues arising from our visits was the lack of material on disability and sexuality in schools (both special and mainstream). Using sex education resources which do not feature disabled people reinforces exclusion for disabled students and confirms prejudices in mainstream schools. Most approached issues within a purely biological framework. Students who had transferred into special schools from mainstream education were clearly better informed about issues such as contraception and HIV/Aids, but not in the context of disability. Lack of specific information may leave disabled people without safer sex messages or knowledge of where to get hold of information (Banim *et al.*, 1999).

Deaf students expressed a wish for hearing partners, having internalised the devaluation of deaf culture and fantasised about this as a strategy for reducing barriers. The young women we spoke to talked about the pressure to hide their hearing impairment in the presence of boys. They were also more dependent on their teachers, since a number of their parents (especially fathers) had little sign language to call on for passing on information or values. Deaf students, in particular, voiced awareness of personal risk and the need for input on personal safety and self-defence, but although deaf people are more at risk of sexual abuse than their peers there is a dearth of appropriate therapeutic resources.

Gay and lesbian issues were not addressed openly within the curricula and we speculate that gay and lesbian disabled students find it more difficult to access out-of-school services such as helplines or networks. Nor were issues of celibacy and/or a single lifestyle portrayed as a positive choice.

But there were more subtle omissions as well. Young disabled people have a keen sense of ethics, which they were not being allowed to voice or develop. At the time of some of our visits a prominent soap opera had dealt with the issue of abortion of a disabled foetus, and the students were very interested in the issues.

Some innovative projects had been set up in community settings. For example, disabled young people enrolled on an employment programme were offered voluntary sessions on sex and sexuality. Other initiatives had not been so successful. A group of day centre users had requested a group to be established to explore sexuality, but although a couple of meetings were held it was dissolved due to apparent lack of interest. Hiccups are inevitable, and services need to give themselves permission to get things wrong without giving up.

There was a plea from members of the core group for local discussion groups to be made available outside the immediate structures of day and residential services – groups which could enable disabled people to overcome this dearth of information and also provide a space where they might meet potential partners and/or helpers. One young woman spoke of her wish to have help in masturbating, but was confused because the staff person she had approached said that this would be outside her contract and might make her liable for dismissal. While the core group (particularly the women) were keenly aware of the risks of abuse, many disabled people want to take more chances, not fewer. Staff cannot fill, but should be alert to, the gaps in people's lives, because they do need to facilitate access to outside bodies (figuratively and literally!) to address these.

The cost of the service

Costs also present a potential barrier, especially to disabled people living on benefits. The costs of services may be met from one of a number of sources:

- the local authority
- the health authority

- disability and incapacity benefits paid direct to the claimant
- payment from the local authority, authorised under the *Direct Payments Act 1996*
- grant-aid or funding paid to a voluntary organisation
- the individual client.

Payment was not an issue in seeking to access many services, although the take-up of counselling services was an important exception. One of the specialist counselling services we visited was free to everyone, but is currently reviewing this policy in favour of a sliding scale of charges for all consultations.

> ### *Key messages*
>
> 1. **Mainstream services which provide counselling and support around sexuality, relationships, sexual and reproductive health and sexual and other abuse need to give further attention to issues of access, acceptability and presentation in order to ensure that their services are as available to disabled people as they are to other groups within the community. They may need to invest in disability equality training to make this a reality; they certainly need to base their services in accessible buildings, to have accessible publicity and to signal clearly that they provide a service to disabled people.**
>
> 2. **Counselling is not consistently available to people with different impairments. People**

> **with severe impairments or with impaired communication are often excluded, and there are not enough counsellors trained to work within a social model of disability. Counselling training should routinely include disability awareness, and services need to develop their expertise in addressing individual needs, exploring joint working and developing ways of working through interpreters where this is indicated.**
>
> 3. **Access to counselling and information services is also geographically patchy: there are islands of excellence within a sea of indifference. Service commissioners should map local resources and/or delegate this task and ensure that they commission new disabled-led services to work within or alongside local networks.**

Staff roles which emphasise assistance

Staff roles are needed which focus on assistance rather than on 'care' or 'control', and which rest on appropriate recruitment, training and support, within clear contracts, and an explicit values base.

Disabled people have established the principle that they should recruit their own personal assistants, and mechanisms have been set up to make this a reality. For example, in one scheme the agency was committed to open advertising when an appropriate PA could not be identified from the available 'pool'. The disabled person then sat as an equal partner on the interviewing panel. In most specialist disability organisations, it would be unusual for disabled people not to be central in the recruitment and selection process, but this principle was less adhered to in the larger charities or in generic agencies. Agencies which have not invested in strong links with disability networks are less likely to be able to access people to sit on panels and may be less committed to inclusion of disabled people than to other marginal and disadvantaged groups identified within equal opportunities policies.

The professional qualities and experience sought in staff seeking to work with disabled people will depend on their duties. Personal qualities will include understanding and acceptance of the social model of disability and evidence that the prospective staff member focuses on the person rather than their impairment. Disabled people and their networks do not want staff who are poorly paid or supported, but are often unable to influence the parameters which affect these outcomes.

Commitment to training

Induction and in-house training were provided within most workplaces, but the extent to which these focused on sex and sexuality varied. Stand-alone courses have been offered by a number of the services visited, from organisations such as SPOD and Relate. There was, however, strong evidence that further training would be welcomed in this area but there was limited knowledge as to where and how to identify training and trainers to meet the need of the service. For example, a member of the core group who undertook a couple of visits was asked by both establishments whether he would be available to offer sexuality training to the staff teams. Some form of 'clearing-house' for accredited trainers would facilitate this process.

Examples of training are given below:

- **FPA training** In 1998/1999 the FPA was running a number of training courses around the UK that focused on sex, sexuality and the personal development of people with profound and multiple impairment. A key plank of the FPA's training in this area was a pack called *Walk Your Talk: Exploring Sexuality and Disability*.

- **Local authority staff training** Each local authority sets its own priorities for guidance and training on these issues. For instance, Kent SSD produced guidelines for good practice for its staff working with disabled people which were used as a starting-point for training with all staff in residential and domiciliary care settings. Initial feedback indicated that staff welcomed the opportunity to talk about some of the situations they faced. From these training sessions a small booklet on good practice was produced for wider circulation. A review system was built into the guidelines so that they can be regularly reviewed and further training provided.

- **Relate** In the autumn of 1997, Relate offered all its volunteer psychotherapists the opportunity to participate in a series of six workshops on sexuality and disability, called 'Neutered No More'. It was the intention to extend this offer to all counsellors in the next year. The aims of the course were:

  - to raise awareness of sexuality issues for disabled people
  - to 'challenge the way in which society defines those disabilities and to build the therapist's confidence'
  - to 'develop knowledge and create enthusiasm for working with this client group'.

- **SPOD** Provides training events both in its London office and, on request, to agencies and establishments around the country. The courses are participative and focus on exploring participants' own attitudes to sexuality rather than on disability issues and politics. Often the trainer reported being hemmed in by ambivalent attitudes to sex, as, for example, when courses were set up for direct care staff but not attended by more senior managers or when they were set up with conditions like 'not talking about sex outside marriage'. Hence buying in a training course may not signal a real commitment to change unless it is seen as one part of a more strategic approach.

- **SCOPE** (in the North East) runs a regular programme of training on sexual issues for staff covering topics such as HIV and Aids, contraception and sexual health. Although this training did relate these issues to disability, it did so largely within a medical rather than a social model.

These training events are all useful ways of raising awareness, but may stop short of achieving much-needed change in service delivery. They require follow-through and a commitment to change at all levels of the service. Bringing in outsiders gives a mixed message: their independence and expertise may be welcomed, but the 'lone ranger' model also implies that sexuality is somehow different from other training within the organisation. It may be seen as less important or as a personal and optional interest rather than a key area of management competence. Reactive as opposed to strategic approaches tended to hold sway. One-off training events are often predicated on the basis that change can be effected by challenging individual staff attitudes (to sex, but not necessarily to disability), and this can be misleading. Staff may feel that, having explored and clarified their own values, they are entitled to impose these on service users. In fact, sexuality issues need to be embedded in much broader strategies for change and disability equality which have as their goal the fullest empowerment of service users. Disabled trainers and consultants should be used more widely to design and deliver this training and to lead service development in this area.

Support and supervision

Although formal training on sexuality was not universally available to staff in many establishments, regular support group meetings were frequently used to explore appropriate responses to situations that arose in the workplace. For example, in a service providing personal assistants, one of the monthly meetings had been used to explore what an appropriate response would be to a disabled client who asked for their involvement in procuring a prostitute. The manager did not rule out the possibility that her staff might facilitate this, but was also willing to explore the boundaries of what they felt comfortable with. Individual supervision sessions and/or staff meetings were also used to discuss issues which were deemed to be too sensitive to convey in a written policy, issues which they assumed were liable to be unacceptable or misunderstood by senior managers and trustees who are far removed from the daily lives of disabled people. One such topic was facilitation of masturbation, the circumstances in which this would be acceptable and what procedures were needed to safeguard everyone involved.

The core group challenged the notion that senior people should be protected from these issues or that staff working directly with disabled people should be left in a double bind, whereby, their livelihoods are at risk if they act to support disabled people around sexual issues.

Policies and procedures

Written policies and procedures cut across the taboo which surrounds the sexual activity of disabled people, especially when they are in receipt of services (day, domiciliary and residential care). We found a number of policy statements including:

- policies on sexuality and relationships, in which such issues as parental involvement, consent and confidentiality are addressed
- policies that strictly forbid relationships between residents and staff, which would result in the dismissal of the latter
- risk assessment policies
- sexual abuse policies
- guidance to male staff about avoiding unfounded allegations of sexual abuse
- policies setting out an ideal of same-sex intimate care
- policies that emphasise that all contact must be of 'a professional nature'
- policies that proscribe staff from retaliating verbally or physically to 'threats, risks, physical abuse or sexual harassment from clients' but no suggestions for appropriate responses to homophobic, sexist or racist comments of or by disabled people
- policies and procedures which govern the recording of counselling sessions
- equal opportunities and health and safety policies.

Part Four Working towards good practice

We did not find examples of policies which advocate unequivocally for the rights and autonomy of disabled people in sexual matters. Work needs to be done to develop and refine model policies and contracts. Policies need to spell out the principle of autonomy and within that make clear to what extent staff are expected to facilitate sexual activity/relationships. Guidance should clearly set out what sexual contact is permissible between disabled people using services and staff, and what is expected of staff as facilitators of sexual acts between disabled people and their chosen partners.

Senior managers and trustees need to take responsibility for difficult areas of practice. That is their job. Otherwise staff who work directly with disabled people (who are often the least paid but most committed) carry the weight of society's ambivalence unfairly and uncomfortably on their shoulders.

> *Key messages*
>
> 1. **Restrictions on community care budgets and payments for independent living, over-use of agency staff and low staffing in residential care cut across the wishes of disabled people to employ staff who are properly paid and supported, with entitlement to sickness and holiday pay and proper job security.**
>
> 2. **There is a lack of both formal and informal accountability in many organisations, as trustees and managers turn away from contentious issues or shy away from stated principles when these are tested in relation**

> to sexual relationships and activities. Written policies, guidance and explicit contracts with staff are needed to ensure that staff can be properly accountable to disabled people and that this responsibility is shared throughout the organisations which serve them.
>
> 3. **Independent advocacy, advice and information should be made available in residential and day care settings so that disabled people are helped to access sexual information, opportunities and partners beyond the immediate circle of those who provide daily assistance to them.**

Review and openness

These can be achieved through listening and learning from internal and external feedback.

Monitoring and evaluation rely on the kind of clarity and involvement set out in the earlier criteria. We did not find many services in which independent evaluations had been carried out or in which routine monitoring was being used to improve service delivery. Inspection units already have powers to recruit lay inspectors and disabled people's networks should be accessed to provide suitable people.

One evaluation which did provide a model had been carried out by Gerry Zarb and Mike Oliver of the Tower Hamlets Counselling Service, which mapped its referral pattern and provision against stated aims and used an explicit social model of disability as a reference point.

SPOD maintains a strict policy of keeping no historical records and is very careful to work within the *Data Protection Act* with its working files. Many of the people who access their service do so because it is separate and 'anonymous', and this is respected. But this stance may also disadvantage the organisation when it comes to reviewing use of its service, and inevitably leads to planning on the basis of incomplete information. For example, monitoring of use by disabled people from ethnic minorities would ensure that their needs could be planned for.

Increasingly, as disabled-led services enter into negotiations for contracts and funding, they will need to be able to demonstrate their effectiveness against clear targets and written policies.

Complaints procedures are also an important source of feedback. Disabled people who are independent should be appointed to panels to hear complaints. Policies on abuse of vulnerable adults may result in allegations of abuse which need to be investigated within an inter-agency framework set up in relation to all adult service users. But these must be tempered by acknowledgement of the autonomy of disabled people and include sensitive assessment of vulnerability or exploitation. Where policies are too rigid complaints may not surface (Wood, 1995), thereby depriving the service of an opportunity to learn.

We hope that the criteria set out in this report will facilitate independent and in-house evaluations of service delivery, embracing both the implications of current service provision for the sexual options of disabled people and the effectiveness of specialist services which exist to support them.

Key messages

1. **Disabled people should be included on complaints panels and as lay inspectors/regulators.**

2. **Clear policy guidelines and statements about how sexual issues are to be dealt with in services should be published by service agencies and form part of the contract with commissioners and care managers.**

3. **Internal and external groups should be encouraged to audit service provision and its implications for disabled people in terms of their sexual options and lives, using criteria derived from a social model of disability and an understanding of disability equality issues.**

Part Five
Some tools for change

In this section we provide some tools for change.

First, we provide you with a light-hearted way of plotting your own and your service's attitudes to sexuality and disability, using a grid to explore how inclusive you are in relation to the issues discussed in this report.

Second, we provide a template which will help you to audit your own service and prioritise some next steps.

Third, we outline some headings which might help you to structure a policy document which is specific to your setting and the issues which arise in that context.

These tools provide the questions, but not the answers, which need to be explored and arrived at after debate and discussion with local disability networks, service users and other interested groups.

Part Five Some tools for change

Where do you stand on issues of sexuality and disability? The inclusiveness grid

Because it is an unusual thing to be asked to help someone else in private areas of their lives, it is important to think about your values and why you hold them. You may be put in situations which challenge you to overcome long-held but unexamined convictions or knee-jerk (dis)approvals. You may, because you know what feels right for *you*, think that you know what is right for others... but then again you may change your mind!

The following light-hearted grid may help you as a citizen, worker or service agency to recognise where you are starting from in relation to these issues. It sets out to map overlapping attitudes to sexuality and disability. The positions on the grid are rather a caricature, but they may help you to see scope for movement in your own attitudes or your service's value base.

If you hold 'exclusive' attitudes to sexuality you will probably be starting from a position that only some things are 'normal' and/or 'natural'. You may think that people should be sexual only if they are independent or if they are married or in a certain type of relationship. More inclusive views accept that people's sexual tastes, practices and sexual orientation are influenced by many factors and that as long as they are consenting and respectful in their sexual relationships and encounters their rights should be upheld.

If you hold exclusive attitudes to disability you are likely to see disabled people as fundamentally different and to exaggerate how normal you and others are by comparison. You may have quite rigid ideas about attractiveness and believe that people should work hard to 'keep up

Inclusive about Disability

The sex aids and implants approach *'This should help you to perform as if you were normal, here are some sex aids... if it isn't hurting it isn't working'*	**Proud visibility** *'You set the agenda... we will help in so far as you want us to... we recognise your right to find your own way and celebrate your sexuality in proud and maybe even shocking ways'*
EXCLUSIVE ABOUT SEXUALITY	INCLUSIVE ABOUT SEXUALITY
Ostrich position *'You must be joking. Sex isn't for the likes of you... you'd have to leave this place for a start'*	**Only beautiful people need apply** *'We only want beautiful people here... this is our scene and you have to be young, fit and thin before we let you in'*

Exclusive about Disability

appearances' by dressing carefully, working out and using cosmetics. More inclusive views would acknowledge a continuum of 'imperfections' and vulnerabilities and a more flexible view of what is healthy and who looks good.

Where exclusive values about both sexuality and disability overlap you or your service are likely to see sex in narrow terms and risk excluding disabled people from 'normal' relationships on account of their impairments. You may even perpetuate the taboos which the disabled people in our core group have lived under in traditional, segregated and institutional services.

If you have more inclusive views about disabled people but still a conservative and narrow view of sex, you are likely to take a kind of assimilationist view and 'allow' people to have some kinds of sexual relationships as long as they are independent and manage without assistance. You might advocate the use of sex aids or other (quite painful) interventions that will help the disabled person to perform as if they are 'normal'.

If you hold inclusive or radical views about sexual politics but negative ones about disabled people, you may well approve of all kinds of sexual practices and relationships or associate yourself with a swinging scene and consumer 'style', even where this excludes of disabled people.
For example, you may condone the 'body beautiful' entry criteria of the gay scene or operate other fixed measures of sexual worth like slimness or youthfulness.

If you have broad, flexible and inclusive views in relation to sexuality and disability, you will be able to include and acknowledge the 'proud visibility' of disabled people and of all those who seek to be sexual whether in traditional or innovative contexts and relationships.

Part Five Some tools for change

Using the six Rs to review your service

In this section, we provide a template to help you use the six Rs to audit and develop your own service provision around sexuality for disabled people or to focus your feedback to a service which you use or have contact with.

You can use the framework to help you crystallise your own views or, better still, to structure a group discussion or staff meeting with others. You could also use the framework as an agenda to guide you in the context of a user–consultation exercise, or a briefing to your management or trustee group.

You may copy the pro-forma without restriction and you will need a supply of felt-tipped pens in red, amber and green to record the outcome of your discussions. You may want to copy pages 15–21 as a handout where the issues addressed by the six Rs framework are set out in detail.

Using these pointers and your own impressions, together with evidence from consumer surveys, records of inquiries, feedback forms and so on, try to reach a consensus about whether you are a:

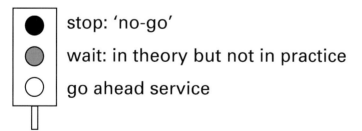

stop: 'no-go'

wait: in theory but not in practice

go ahead service

in relation to sexuality and related areas of practice. You can refer back to the way we categorised these 'positions' on pages 9–14.

Part Five Some tools for change

1. A Rights Perspective

🔴 Sexual options for disabled people are limited because powerful groups, such as founder members, parent/carer groups, fundraising committees, staff or managers might not approve.

🔴 Sexual rights are recognised in theory but little practical assistance is offered and disabled people are not actively helped to access information or support from outside the service and/or their immediate network.

🔴 Sexual rights are recognised, respected and planned for. Autonomy is the key principle and controversial decisions are supported unless there are explicit concerns about exploitation of or by others. Disabled people are actively helped to express their sexuality in whatever ways they choose.

2. Role Models

🔴 Your service is largely professionally based and you do not have, or particularly seek, disabled people as staff or volunteers.

🔴 You have made half-hearted efforts to involve disabled people, but the extra support needed is privately regarded as a bit of a chore. A few disabled people in 'token' positions is all you have achieved.

🔴 You involved disabled people as staff (including in management roles) volunteers and outside consultants/visitors. Where your work is with young people you provide opportunities for them to meet and learn from

88 © Pavilion Publishing/Joseph Rowntree Foundation, 2000

older disabled adults. Where your work is with adults you encourage and support generic and specialist disability networks (such as those growing up around gay and lesbian disabled people and around disabled people from ethnic minorities). You encourage the arts and have great pictures of disabled people around to provide a positive atmosphere.

3. User Responsibility

🔴 Your service is mainly run by professionals and you have not made any plans to employ disabled people as staff or trainers, nor do you involve disabled people in decision-making groups. Disabled people who use your service are not consulted or encouraged to make decisions about the service or its response to sexual or other controversial issues.

🟡 Your service is committed to user involvement in theory. You have a user committee or similar group which meets regularly but it does not have many teeth when it comes to challenging the way the service is run. You advertise yourself as an equal opportunity employer but you don't get many applicants for some reason and you haven't been able to find new ways of involving people as yet.

🟢 You support the involvement of disabled people at all levels of your organisation. Your organisation is largely managed by disabled people whose influence is guaranteed through your agency's written constitution. In relation to sexuality you ensure that you have disabled trainers and educators to call on and disabled people are represented on groups to which you refer difficult ethical dilemmas.

Part Five Some tools for change

4. Inclusiveness Across a Range of Services

🔴 Your premises are not accessible and you make no
⚪ special arrangements in your publicity to attract
⚪ disabled people as clients or to indicate that your
service would meet their needs.

⚪ Your services are accessible but you do not represent
🔴 disabled people in your literature or publicity material
⚪ or produce material in a range of formats to meet the
needs of people with communication, visual or hearing
impairments.

⚪ Your service is in accessible premises and your
⚪ publicity material makes it clear that you value disabled
🔴 people as service users and workers. Material is
available in a range of formats, including audio, Braille
and large print. It features disability issues in its contents.
You have Minicom for people to ring in and your
reception staff have been trained in disability
awareness.

5. Staff Roles Which Emphasise Assistance Not 'Care'

🔴 Staff see themselves in a traditional caring, almost
⚪ 'parenting' role which entitles them to give advice and
⚪ make decisions on behalf of the disabled people they
serve. Some staff are low-paid and have not had much
training.

⚪ Staff are committed to choice and autonomy but are
🔴 afraid to let go in practice. They are bound by policies
⚪ and by a culture which holds them responsible for

things which are controversial and they are wary of letting disabled people make mistakes. They don't see helping with sexual relationships or activity as part of their job at all. Staff have had training but this has focused on their own attitudes and values and not those of the disabled person they serve.

Staff have a contract which sets out their role in terms of assistance, and sexual activity is clearly identified within this as a legitimate support need. Staff give sensitive, practical help without necessarily approving of the disabled person's actions, but which they respect as 'their business'.

6. Review and Openness

Your service is quite closed and you do not have many visitors or people enquiring into the way you run it. As far as you are concerned things run smoothly and you do not see a need to change for change's sake.

You are open to suggestions in a limited way if they are offered, but you do not go out of your way to get feedback or find out about new areas of need.

You build in regular reviews of your service which involve consultation with service users and other disabled people and their networks. Some of these evaluations are conducted by independent groups of disabled people who help you to shape your service.

The following statements are designed to help you decide how well you are doing.

Developing a policy document

Policies exist to clarify the role of staff, their responsibilities and duties. Policies alert staff and service users to difficult areas of practice and set out the principles on which decisions should be made. The key principles which apply are:

- autonomy
- recognising unequal power
- respecting privacy and confidentiality.

Procedures exist to set out ways of making decisions, indicating the leeway available to each person as to:

- how they do their job
- what to do about disagreements or complex situations
- what records they keep.

Policies should not 'beat about the bush' when it comes to sex between staff and service users, but spell out whether it is acceptable and, if so, in what circumstances and with what safeguards. In learning disability services the differential in power between staff and service users is deemed to negate valid consent on the part of a service user in any sexual contact with staff and this is defined as abuse in policies and contracts. But in services for disabled people who require physical help and who are able to take their own decisions and responsibilities, the default settings are, and should be, different, and this should be reflected in agency policies.

Staff should also be left in no doubt that supporting

disabled people in their sexual lives is a legitimate part of the job. In interviews and written job descriptions this aspect of the work needs to be spelt out. This would put the onus on staff to claim exemption from assisting disabled people in this area of their lives, rather than on disabled people to keep establishing their right to be sexual. What tends to happen is that the work becomes shrouded in a mist of rhetoric and assistants are left holding uncomfortable, but unacknowledged, feelings which weaken their commitment to the rights of disabled people. For example, policy documents may be constructed around words like 'privacy' or 'confidentiality', when the nub of the issue for staff is that they know things about individuals which they would not normally know and sometimes, in order to behave professionally, they need to discuss these issues with colleagues. This risks cutting across confidentiality so they have to weigh up two competing principles: that of confidentiality and that of responsible information-sharing.

You can construct a policy document by using the following headings as a focus for debate and consultation.

Headings for a model policy

Your remit

- How does your service impact on the sexual options of disabled people? In other words, what are you there to do or provide? (It is important to be specific; for example, if you provide accommodation it will be clear that you do not need to provide spiritual counsel as part of the tenancy.)

Whom do you serve?

- Is your service inclusive, or does it aim to support one group more than others or to provide assistance around a specific set of issues (such as HIV/Aids)?

- Do you have information about who has used your service in the past? For example, if you provide services to a general population, how do you know how many disabled people you have served and how many potential customers you have with disabilities?

- Begin by defining the group you serve and making a clear distinction between the issues for people who may lack capacity to consent to sexual activity or who are not able to manage complex decisions about their own lives (such as people with learning disabilities or brain damage) and those disabled people whose need is for practical assistance to support their own autonomous decision-making.

Who are your staff and what is their role?

- What support and training needs do your staff have? Where do your staff come from? Do they have a shared background, for example through professional training or culture, which needs addressing at a corporate level, or individual training needs which need to be addressed through one-to-one sessions or mentoring?

- What is the role of staff in supporting and responding to sexuality and sexual expression? Is this set out explicitly in their contracts and conditions of employment?

- What do you expect staff <u>not</u> to do in their relationships with disabled people? Have you debated these rules with them openly?

Resolving conflict

- What are the dilemmas which arise in your service and how will difficult decisions be made?

- What forums exist for difficult decisions to be debated and resolved, where, for example, you deem the interests of one service user to be in conflict with those of another?

- How will disabled people influence these judgements? Do you have outside, neutral people to draw on who are members of, or have strong links with, disability networks? If so, what is their task or remit and how are they brought in?

Upholding the sexual rights of disabled people

State the extent to which you will uphold the sexual rights of disabled people using your service. Areas to be covered by agency policies should include:

- opposite and same-sex relationships

- the role of staff in assisting in sexual acts/relationships and their rights to withdraw from this aspect of the work

- respect for autonomy and limits to advice or approval-giving

- sensitivity to cultural and religious differences
- sensitivity to sexual expression in the context of intimate care
- availability of, and access to, empowering sex education
- staff/client relationships and sexual contact, including those between disabled people as employers and their personal assistants
- access to information in relation to HIV and safer sex
- how to access mainstream services such as GUM services, family planning, ante-natal services and rape crisis services
- responses to sexually inappropriate or challenging behaviour
- privacy and confidentiality of personal information.

Policies exist to clarify the principles on which these difficult areas of practice rest. They should begin with autonomy and assuring the civil liberties of disabled people, but acknowledge those areas where conflicts of interest and issues of exploitation may exist.

Procedures exist to set out ways of making decisions, indicating the leeway available to each person as to:

- how they do their job
- what to do about disagreements or complex situations
- what records they keep
- what facilities, input and assistance you can put people in touch with; it is always useful to draw together a list of local agencies and sources of assistance.

You will want to document exceptions to the principle

of autonomy which your service has identified before particular issues come to attention. For example, would you uphold the rights of disabled people to act outside the law or expect staff to be in any way involved in assisting such activities as cottaging or smoking a joint after sex? It is in relation to these difficult areas of practice, where differences of opinion are apparent or controversies are likely that you need to define how far your service will go to support civil liberties.

For example you might write:

> 'Tenancies are offered to disabled people regardless of race, sex, culture or sexual orientation. Gay and lesbian tenants are welcome and entitled to the same level of support in their relationships as heterosexual residents. Where possible, gay staff will be employed to assist gay residents and facilitate their involvement in local gay networks.'

or

> 'Although the values of this organisation do not accord with the use of pornography, we acknowledge the right of adults over 18 to access and use such material. We ask them to use it in their own private space (ie their bedrooms) and not in communal areas where it might offend other residents, staff or visitors.'

Part Six
Summary of key messages

1. A model of disability and sexuality which focuses on social processes such as expectations, imagery and barriers is more useful than one which dwells on individual impairments and biological differences.

2. Young disabled people should not be disadvantaged in their relationships or compromised in their autonomy. They should be helped to access disabled adults who can help them develop a strong sense of their identity as disabled people.

3. Openness and explicitness, however awkward, should be the goal, so that individual members of staff who support disabled people who need assistance are not left unprotected and unsupported.

4. Users should be involved in the design and governance of services wherever possible, and particularly in those aspects of service which impact upon the freedoms of disabled people in their personal and sexual relationships. To this end, disability equality training (which also addresses sexual rights) should be available on a regular basis for mainstream organisations, planners and commissioners and non-disabled management committees.

Part Six Summary of key messages

5. Agencies serving disabled people need to employ disabled people throughout their organisations and particularly in roles which directly support disabled people in their emotional and sexual lives; role models and life experiences are important alongside more orthodox qualifications. Training for disabled people to assume these roles should be developed and funded.

6. Disabled people who are appointed to management committees or as members of staff should be accorded equal status and assured an equal say in decision-making bodies and staff teams.

7. Mainstream services which provide counselling and support around sexuality, relationships, sexual and reproductive health and experiences of abuse need to attend to issues of access, acceptability and presentation in order to ensure that their services are as available to disabled people as they are to other groups within the community. They may need to invest in disability equality training to make this a reality. Services certainly need to be provided in accessible buildings, to have accessible publicity and to signal clearly that they are open to disabled people.

8. Counselling is not consistently available to people with different impairments – people with severe impairments or with impaired communication are often excluded – nor are there enough counsellors trained to work within a social model of disability. Counselling training should routinely include disability awareness and services need to develop their expertise in addressing individual need, exploring joint working and developing ways of working through interpreters where this is indicated.

9. Access to counselling and information services is also geographically patchy. There are islands of excellence within a sea of indifference. Service commissioners should map local resources and/or delegate this task and ensure that they commission new disabled-led services to work within or alongside local networks.

10. Restrictions on community care budgets and payments for independent living, over-use of agency staff and low staffing in residential care cut across the wishes of disabled people to employ staff who are properly paid and supported, with entitlement to sick and holiday pay and proper job security.

11. There is a lack of both formal and informal accountability in many organisations, as trustees and managers shield themselves from contentious issues or shy away from stated principles when these are publicly tested in relation to sexual relationships and activities. Written guidance and explicit contracts with funding bodies and with individual staff are needed to ensure that staff can be properly accountable to disabled people and that this responsibility is shared throughout the organisations which serve them.

12. Independent advocacy, advice and information should be made available in residential and daycare settings so that disabled people are helped to access sexual information, opportunities and partners beyond the immediate circle of those who provide daily assistance to them.

13. Disabled people should be included on complaints panels and as lay inspectors/regulators.

14. Clear policy guidelines and statements about how sexual issues are to be dealt with in services should be published by service agencies and form part of the contract with commissioners and care managers.

15. Internal and external groups should be encouraged to audit service provision and its implications for disabled people in terms of their sexual options and lives, using criteria derived from a social model of disability and an understanding of disability equality issues.

Part Seven
How we worked together

Disabled people doing research, not being researched

Disabled academics and activists have developed a powerful analysis of the unequal 'social relations' which underlie the agenda, conduct and dissemination of many research projects and the exploitation of the experiences of disabled people as 'subjects' of this research.

Research methodologies and values are contested in all social sciences, but the disabled community has articulated this challenge particularly strongly. Both quantitative and qualitative approaches carry the potential for misuse of power, lack of participation and hidden biases behind the supposed neutrality/objectivity of the researchers (Oliver, 1992). Consultation with disabled people as to the research agenda and its purposes (Oliver, 1992) has led to the formulation of a more radical agenda, *'which places people with disabilities and their concerns centre stage at every point in research process aimed at facilitating their empowerment'* (Ward & Flynn, 1994, p31).

Radical research favours user-led processes and agendas and user control over the processes of conceptualisation and data gathering (Rachmaran & Grant, 1994). This is not to argue that disabled people do not need research deriving from different disciplines and approaches, or that professionals do not have a place in conducting research.

But it is important that researchers seek to address the issues which disabled people place at the top of their agenda rather than to further knowledge without at least the potential for changing lives.

This project did not completely match up to these aspirations. It was the non-disabled academics who defined the framework for the initial proposal, but they then worked closely with the core group in setting the agenda, visiting and consulting services and amending drafts of this report. There was a shared commitment to document the analysis of disabled people rather than the unaccountable views of the authors. The task was defined as the collation of ideas and findings made by the disabled consultants who made up the core group, rather than research on them, their experiences, attitudes or contact with services.

The methodology

The work was conducted through a partnership between a core group of ten people and a research team of four people. All the members of the core group identified themselves as disabled, as did one member of the project team.

Five research approaches were woven together:

- the development of a shared analysis by the core group through their participation at four meetings
- the development of criteria for good practice in the field of sex and sexuality through discussion and debate at these meetings

- visits to agencies and services offering support, information and advice to facilitate disabled people in the arena of sexual activity and sexuality
- review of documentation, policies and training packs
- the production, negotiation and dissemination of this report.

Visits undertaken by members of the core group and the research team were planned to complement the knowledge and analysis of the core group. Supplementary material was reviewed and phone conversations were also carried out to test out the usefulness of the criteria we had drawn up and to identify the dilemmas which arise when a sexual rights perspective is used as the basis of practice.

The core group was drawn together to represent different experiences, expertise and professional backgrounds. It contained men and women...

- who were either born with an impairment or had acquired an impairment in later life
- with different sexual preferences
- from metropolitan, urban and rural areas
- from different ethnic communities
- with diverse life experiences in terms of age (22–55), upbringing, relationships and family responsibilities
- who had current experience of living in the community and/or in residential care
- who had followed different career and social paths
- who were employed by, or were members of, disability networks and related agencies.

The group were not, however, representative of all disabled people; in many respects they were atypical in the resources they brought to the task. Many work within an explicitly political model of disability (with a small 'p'!), and as such they have a strong sense of themselves as disabled individuals and as part of the Disability Movement. Other disabled people might indeed feel more isolated and unsupported. Beresford and Campbell (1994) have explored different meanings attached to the experience of 'representativeness' (p316). They point out that representatives may not be typical and that the very act of representing other disabled people and of having one's views heard and challenged may make people in this position more confident (p317):

> 'Getting involved may not only lead to change, but also change us. We become different. We become 'unrepresentative' in ways some service providers do not want. We become confident, experienced, informed and effective.'

We thought it was important to remember that not all disabled people are linked into disability networks or strengthened by a sense of shared identity and action.

> **'I see many disabled people and newly disabled people who are not in disability politics and can't bring themselves to call themselves disabled. This needs to be understood.'**

The core group were central to the project through:

- the sharing of their own experiences, expertise and analysis gleaned from their direct contact with disability networks and services, thereby contributing to a grounded view of relevant practice issues
- the development and negotiation of agreed criteria against which good practice could be evaluated
- the identification of relevant services, agencies and documentation which could inform this project
- visiting some of these agencies with members of the project team to review service provision and discuss issues with users and staff
- advising in the production of the final report.

The development of criteria for good practice

One of the early tasks of the core group was to agree and endorse the criteria for good practice set out on pages 15–21. This was achieved by the close of the second meeting. A next stage was to identify the kinds of service which impact on the sexuality and sexual options of individual disabled people. Our criteria were then used as a yardstick when reviewing those services with users and staff.

Approximately twenty visits and meetings were organised. Most of the services we contacted had made definite attempts to address issues around sexuality and personal relationships and/or were working to develop good practice. We contacted agencies providing services to different target groups of disabled people, including services for young people, several larger organisations for disabled people, some mainstream agencies providing counselling and advice and some organisations and networks run by disabled people themselves. We were limited in time and resources, making geography and accessibility factors in our selection. We were under no illusions that this was a representative sample or that lessons could be generalised across different geographical areas, types of service and/or organisational structures. But we did attempt to contact a wide range of agencies and to explore how far their agendas reflected the indicators we had drawn up.

Wherever possible, a member of the research team and the core group visited services together. The criteria set by the core group provided the backdrop for the meeting, but the nature of the establishment or service influenced the style and content of the discussion. Service users were consulted in some services, while in others contact was only with staff who were not, in the main, disabled themselves. We also collected and reviewed some written documents from these and other agencies, such as training manuals, information packs, leaflets and policy documents.

Although this report has been written by the research team, the core group have been consulted at different stages of its production and have commented on and amended the text of successive drafts.

Part Eight
Acknowledgments

The core group

The core group met four times during the course of the project. The meetings were held in London. The agendas were circulated in advance and the meetings were chaired by a member of the research team. Discussion was informal, but notes were taken and some parts of the meetings taped, so that transcripts could be made. Participation was facilitated by the sensitivity of the group to the communication needs of each individual. The four meetings had a different focus:

Meeting 1 February 1997

Covered introductions to each person's experiences, expertise and participation needs and began to document personal and professional experience in this area and identify key issues/analyses.

Meeting 2 April 1997

Moved on to consider service needs and to consolidate the group's aspirations for service agencies. It was from these two discussions that a draft set of criteria was drawn up.

Part Eight Acknowledgments

Meeting 3 October 1997

Reviewed these criteria and considered some issues arising from the literature. More detailed discussion of ethical issues and controversies took place at this meeting.

Meeting 4 February 1998

Focused on the draft report, debating the scope and voice of the report and its key messages.

The group is thanked for the high level of commitment and the lively and challenging nature of their debates on which this report is based.

Membership of the group was as follows.

Clive Bassant

Clive lives independently in the Kent area and manages his own care package. He is Deputy Manager of Chatham Citizen's Advice Bureau and sits on the Council of the British Coalition of Disabled People (BCODP). He campaigns nationally for disability rights and is a member of REGARD, the network of gay and lesbian disabled people which is actively challenging disempowerment within both disability and gay and lesbian movements.

Frances Blackwell

Frances Blackwell is a psychotherapist registered with the United Kingdom Committee for Psychotherapy and is a Member of the Institute of Psychotherapy and Social Studies, London. Her background was social work and counselling, and she has been a disability equality trainer and now works for the Disability Counselling Service in Tower Hamlets Health Trust.

Petra Greenaway

Petra spent her childhood in Jamaica and 'escaped' from residential care as an adult, despite the expectations of the staff and of the church. She belongs to the Black Disabled People's Group and campaigns for greater awareness of the needs of Black disabled people.

Yvonne Hall

Yvonne lives independently with her partner whom she married while they were both living in residential care. She has been on the board of SHAD and is an expert on housing issues for disabled people. She has pursued her interest in politics through studying for an MA.

Mildrette Hill

Millie Hill was born in 1957 in Bermuda but was brought up in America and Canada. She broke her neck in a diving accident when she was 14. She was a professional journalist for a number of years, had a degree in law and practised as a barrister. She was the founder of the Black Disabled People's Group which was set up to address the problem of under-representation of Black people in society in general and specifically within the disability movement. She died in 1997. She wrote about her life in 'Patricia's mother', one of the contributions in Lois Keith's edited collection of writing by disabled women entitled *Mustn't Grumble,* published by Women's Press in 1995.

Alison John

Alison is a member of the Parent-ability network which supports disabled people around becoming parents and parenting issues. She is a qualified social worker and experienced youth worker.

Margaret Kennedy

Margaret Kennedy is a disability and child protection trainer and consultant. Choosing to specialise in disabled children who are abused, she is the co-editor and co-author of the 'ABCD' pack (*Abuse and Children who are Disabled: Training and resource pack*). She writes and trains nationally and internationally in this area, including sexual and emotional abuse of disabled children, investigative interviews with non-speaking disabled children, safe residential practice and bullying of disabled and deaf children. She founded and ran the 'Keep deaf children safe' project for six years. Her other interests include work around professionals and clergy who abuse their clients, as part of which she works with Christian survivors of abuse and trains on Christianity and abuse. She is a member of the editorial board of the *Journal of Adult Protection*.

Peter Mansell

At the time of writing, Peter Mansell was the Executive Director of the Spinal Injuries Association (SIA). He has had a longstanding interest in social policy issues and disability politics since becoming disabled through a road traffic accident in his 20s. He has participated in various networks and organisations both for and of disabled people, such as the National Disabled Workers Group of the Citizens Advice Bureaux, Scope, the Disability Resource Team, the Alliance of Disability Advice and Information Providers and SIA. Peter is a member of the British Council of Disabled People. Peter holds a BA (Hons) as well as a diploma in management and specialises in management of not-for-profit organisations. He is married with two sons and lives in London.

Saadia Neilson

Saadia is an independent trainer/consultant around disability, race, child protection and domestic violence issues. She has worked for social service departments, voluntary organisations, education authorities and development agencies throughout the UK. She is a certified associate of the IPD and a founder member of the first national organisation of Black disabled people in Britain – Black Spectrum.

Simon Parrit

A chartered counselling psychologist with a special interest in relationships, sexuality and disability, Simon is a senior lecturer and supervisor with the Institute of Sexuality and Human Relations and works part-time for Hammersmith and Fulham Action for Disability as a counselling psychologist. He is a visiting lecturer at the Maudesley Hospital course in couple relationship and sex therapy and has recently taken over as Director of SPOD, having been its Vice-Chair for several years.

Kerry Parsons

Kerry Parsons is 22 and lives in the Leonard Cheshire Home in Gloucestershire. She has cerebral palsy. Since living in

Cheltenham she has become involved in two research projects: one about living in residential care, and this one about sexuality. She uses the Lifestyles service, which is a group organised for disabled people aged 16–65 to improve the quality of their social lives, and also enjoys going to see shows and musicals. In the future she is going to take part in the Prince's Trust, which will be a challenge to broaden her horizons.

Through the core group the project was able to access the experience of the following networks, services and agencies:

- Tower Hamlets Counselling Service for Disabled People
- Spinal Injuries Association
- Parent-ability
- REGARD (Gay and Lesbian network)
- SPOD (the association to aid the sexual and personal relationships of people with a disability)
- SHAD (housing support agency).

The research team

Hilary Brown

Until recently Hilary was Professor of Social Care at the School of Health and Social Welfare, Open University and now holds an honorary post there. She currently works as a consultant in social care at Salomons, which is a faculty within Canterbury Christ Church University College. She has a longstanding interest in issues of sexuality and gender in social care services and in abuse/adult protection.

Clare Croft-White

Clare has a background in mental health, drug and alcohol, homelessness and HIV services. She has an MBA and is a freelance consultant specialising in the voluntary sector and in evaluation methodologies. She has worked specifically on projects for women who use services and is committed to user involvement in evaluation and service development. Until recently she also worked for the Department of Health in research administration and she has expertise in fundraising.

June Stein

June is a researcher. Having completed a psychology degree at the University of Kent, she has specialised in work on challenging behaviour, sexual abuse and adult protection. In 1997, after six years at the Tizard Centre, University of Kent, she moved to the Open University and holds grants there on family perceptions of abuse and on monitoring systems for adult protection in social services and inspection units.

Christine Wilson

Chris is a freelance disability equality consultant, researcher and trainer. Her active involvement in developing disability equality training alongside other disabled people led her to provide training for trainers in England, Scotland and Ireland. Some of her recent work has focused on consultancy and research for local authorities seeking to improve services to disabled adults and young people, including youth work provision, voluntary organisations seeking mergers and the devising of a disability equality strategy for a lottery distributor. She is also an associate researcher and trainer with the Centre for Social Action at De Montford University, Leicester, working with Unicef in Ukraine on developing a programme for the deinstitutionalisation of young people.

Services visited and consulted

We visited and/or talked to a number of services which included:

- Yorkshire Residential School for the Deaf
- Hereward College, Coventry
- SPOD (the association to aid the sexual and personal relationships of people with a disability)
- Leonard Cheshire Homes
- Scope (formerly the Spastics Society)
- Strode Park
- DISCERN, Nottingham
- Northampton SHARP Project
- Queen Elizabeth Foundation, Kent
- Relate, Rugby
- PHAB

and we would like to thank all those who shared their practice and issues with us.

Other agencies spoke on the phone or sent information and documents, and we would like to extend our thanks to them for their contribution. They included:

- South East Regional Trainers Forum, Canterbury
- FPA Northern Ireland

- APIC Centre, Dublin
- ReABLE, (Relate) Carmarthen
- Gay and Lesbian Group of the MS Society.

Support for the project

The project was administered at the School of Health and Social Welfare of The Open University by Mrs Julie Stock and Mrs Kath Jones. Ms Debbie Stone provided IT support to the project.

Dr Linda Ward of the Joseph Rowntree Foundation has been unfailingly supportive, as have Pavilion staff at ORT House, Camden, for which thanks are due. Mr Peter White and Mr Colin Hughes at the BBC Disabilities Unit also gave encouragement to the project.

Further information

For information on useful and relevant organisations, contact SPOD (the association to aid the sexual and personal relationships of people with a disability) at 286 Camden Road, London N7 0BJ. Tel 020 7607 8851.

References

Banim, M., Guy, A. & Tasker, P. (1999) Trapped in risky behaviour: empowerment, disabled people and sexual health. *Health, Risk and Society,* **1** (2) 209–221.

Bauby, J. C. (1996) *The Diving Bell and the Butterfly.* London: Fourth Estate.

Beresford, P. & Campbell, J. (1994) Disabled people, service users, user involvement and representation. *Disability and Society,* **9** (3).

Bignall, T. & Butt, J. (1999) *Between Ambition and Achievement: Black young disabled people's views and experiences of independence and independent living.* London: Racial Equality Unit.

Brown, H. & Smith, H. (1989) Whose ordinary life is it anyway? *Disability, Handicap and Society,* **4** (2) 105–119.

Clements, J., Clare, I. C. H. & Ezelle, L. A. (1995) Real men, real women, real lives? Gender issues in learning disabilities and challenging behaviour. *Disability and Society,* **10** (4) 425–437.

Connell, R. (1995) *Masculinities.* Cambridge: Polity.

Corbett, J. (1994) A proud label: exploring the relationship between disability politics and gay pride. *Disability and Society,* **9** (3) 343–358.

Craft, A. & Craft, M. (Eds.) (1983) *Sex Education and Counselling for Mentally Handicapped People.* Tunbridge Wells: Costello.

Craft, A. (Ed.) (1987) *Mental Handicap and Sexuality: Issues and perspectives.* Tunbridge Wells: Costello.

Craft, A. (Ed.) (1994) *Practice Issues in Sexuality and Learning Disabilities.* London: Routledge.

Davis, F. (1964) Deviance disavowal: the management of strained interaction by the visibly handicapped. In: S. Becker (Ed.) (1964) *The Other Side.* London: Collier Macmillan.

Dean, J. (1997) The reflective solidarity of democratic feminism. In: J. Dean (Ed.) *Resisting the Political*. London: Sage London.

Doyle, Y. (1995) Disability: use of an independent living fund in South East London and users' views about the system of cash versus care provision. *Journal of Epidemiology and Community Health*, (49) 43–7.

Ducharme, S. (1991) Editorial. *Sexuality and Disability*, **9** (1) 7–8.

Finkelstein,V. (1997) Valedictory Lecture School of Health and Social Welfare, Open University.

Francis, H. (1997) *For Whose Benefit?* Advocacy in Action.

Gillespie-Sells, K., Hill, M. & Robbins, B. (1998) *She Dances to Different Drums: Research into disabled women's sexuality*. London: King's Fund.

Greer, G. (1986) *Sex and Destiny: The politics of fertility*. London: Secker and Warburg.

Goffman, I. (1961) *Stigma: some notes on the management of spoiled identity*. London: Penguin.

Hanna, W. & Rogovky, B. (1991) Women with disabilities: two handicaps plus. *Disability, Handicap and Society*, **6** (1) 49–63.

Hevey, D. (1992) *The Creatures Time Forgot: Philosophy and Disability Imagery*. London: Routledge.

Hevey, D. (1997) *Boo*. Over the Edge, BBC Disabilities Unit (shown on BBC2 Oct 1st 1997).

Hughes, B. & Paterson, K. (1997) The social model of disability and the disappearing body: towards a sociology of impairment. *Disability and Society*, **12** (3) 325–340.

Kaesar, F. (1992) Can people with severe mental retardation consent to mutual sex? *Sexuality and Disability*, **10** (1).

Keith, L. (1994) *'Mustn't Grumble'*: Writing by disabled women. London: Women's Press.

Keith, L. (1997) *A Different Life*. London: Women's Press.

Kuusisto, S. (1998) *Planet of the Blind*. London: Faber & Faber.

Lapper, A. (1997) *Strange Little Creatures*. Over the Edge, BBC Disabilities Unit (shown on BBC2 Oct 15th 1997).

Law Commission (1995) *Mental Incapacity: Item 9 of the Fourth Programme of Law Reform: Mentally Incapacitated Adults*. Law Commission no 231. London: HMSO.

Lennon, P. (1997) The body politic. In: *Guardian Society*, Oct 1st 1997 p9.

Longmore, P. (1987) Screening stereotypes: images of disabled people in television and motion pictures. In: A. Gartner & T. Joe (Eds.) *Images of the Disabled, Disabling Images*. London: Praeger.

Morris, J. (1991) *Pride against Prejudice: Transforming Attitudes to disability*. London: Women's Press.

Morris, J. (1993) Gender and disability. In: J. Swain, V. Finkelstein, S. French & M. Oliver (Eds.) *Disabling Barriers – Enabling environments*. London: Sage.

Noonan-Walsh, P. (1988) Handicapped and female: two disabilities. In: R. McConkey & P. McGinley (Eds.) *Concepts and Controversies in Services for People with Mental Handicap* pp65–82. Dublin: St Michael's House.

Oliver, M. (1990) *The Politics of Disablement*. London: Macmillan.

Oliver, M. (1992) Changing the social relations of research production. *Disability, Handicap and Society*, **7** 101–114.

Pfeiffer, D. (1991) The influence of the socio-economic characteristics of disabled people on their employment status and income. *Disability, Handicap and Society,* **6** (2) 103–115.

Rachmaran, P. & Grant, G. (1994) Setting one agenda for empowering persons with a disadvantage within the research process. In: M. Rioux & M. Bach (Eds.) *Disability is not Measles*. Ontario: Roeher Institute.

Renteria, D. (1993) Rejection. In: R. Luczak (Ed.) *Eyes of Desire: A deaf gay and lesbian reader*. Boston: Alyson.

Shakespeare, T. (1994) Cultural representation of disabled people: dustbins for disavowal. *Disability and Society,* **9** (3) 283–301.

Shakespeare, T., Gillespie-Sells, K. & Davies, D. (1996) *The Sexual Politics of Disability: Untold Desires*. London: Cassell.

Shuttleworth, P. & Redgrove, P. (1978, revised 1986) *The Wise Wound: Menstruation and Everywoman*. London: Paladin.

Stewart, O. (1993) Double oppression: an appropriate starting point? In: J. Swain, V. Finkelstein, S. French & M. Oliver (1993) *Disabling Barriers – Enabling environments*. London: Sage.

Stone, S. (1995) The myth of bodily perfection. *Disability and Society*, **10** (4) 413–424.

Tilley, M. (1996) Sexuality in women with physical disabilities: a social justice or health issue. *Sexuality and Disability,* **14** (2) 139–152.

Townsley, R., Howarth, J., Le Grys., P. & Macadam, M. (1997) *Getting Involved in Choosing Staff*. Brighton: Pavilion Publishing.

Veskner, S. (1993) Bud medicine. In: *Guardian Weekend*, 17 April 1993. Cited in Corbett, J. (1994) A proud label: exploring the relationship between disability politics and gay pride. *Disability and Society,* **9** (3) 343–358.

Ward, L. & Flynn, M. (1994) What matters most: disability, research and empowerment. In: M. Rioux & M. Bach (1994) (Eds.) *Disability is not Measles*. Ontario: Roeher Institute.

Watt, M. (1997) *Working in partnership: involving users and carers in planning community care*. MSc thesis Huddersfield University.

Watson, N. & Shakespeare, T. (1995) Habeamus corpus? Sociology of the body and the issue of impairment. Paper presented to Changing Organisms: Organisms and Change, Quincentennial Conference on the History of Medicine, University of Aberdeen, July 1995.

Weeks, J. (1989) *Sexuality*. London: Routledge.

Winkler, F. (1987) Consumerism in health care: beyond the supermarket model. *Policy and Politics*, 1–8.

White, A. (1996) *Sexuality and Physical Disability*. Report of a conference held on 14th June 1996, SE Regional Trainers Forum c/o Health Promotion Department, Canterbury, Kent.

Wood, D. (1995) *Complaint procedures in mental health services*. SETRHA.

Young, A. Ackerman, J. & Kyle, J. (1998) *Looking On: Deaf people and the organisation of services*. West Sussex: Policy Press.

Zarb, G. & Oliver, M. (1995) *Evaluation of Tower Hamlets Counselling Service for Disabled People* (unpublished report).

Zarb, G. & Nadash, P. (1994) *Cashing in on Independence: Comparing the costs and benefits of cash and services*. BCODP.